UNIQUE EATS AND EATERIES OF MAINE

THE PEOPLE AND STORIES BEHIND THE FOOD

MIKE URBAN

Reedy Press
PO Box 5131
St. Louis, MO 63139, USA
www.reedypress.com

Library of Congress Control Number: 2022949152

ISBN: 9781681064383

Design by Jill Halpin

Photos by author unless otherwise noted.

Printed in the United States of America
23 24 25 26 27   5 4 3 2 1

UNIQUE EATS AND EATERIES OF MAINE

THE PEOPLE AND STORIES BEHIND THE FOOD

MIKE URBAN

Allagash Brewing

DEDICATION

For Sylvia

Central Provisions

CONTENTS

Pemaquid Seafood

ACKNOWLEDGMENTS

Researching and writing this book has been an adventure and a joy, which has been made easier and more fun thanks to the help of many.

First, my thanks and admiration go to the hundreds of restaurant owners and workers at the establishments I've chosen to include in this book. I witnessed firsthand many of their struggles, innovations, and persistence through difficult times—staffing issues, rapidly rising food costs, and so much more—and I'm continually amazed at the perseverance and innovation they've shown throughout. Thanks for all that you do.

Thanks also to friends and colleagues who provided guidance, suggestions, and encouragement along the way. There's Kim Knox Beckius, senior travel editor at *Yankee* magazine, with whom I shared a house in Damariscotta Mills during the summer of 2022, when I performed the bulk of my most recent Maine research. Our landlords, Kevin and Sara Ellis, were gracious hosts, attentive to our every need. Then there are Maine experts Nancy Marshall, Brian Kevin, and Hilary Nangle, who've been unfailingly kind in their assistance and advice. You've all helped make my work a downright pleasure.

And thanks to the staff at Reedy Press for all their support and encouragement during the creation of this book. I continue to be impressed and blessed by all their good work.

And finally, as always, to my wife, Ellen, who held down the fort back in Connecticut while I drove all over Maine, eating, taking pictures, and scratching that Maine itch that I've had for so long. You've got lots of good karma coming your way (including that solo return trip to Europe you've been dreaming about for many years). *Je t'aime, ma chérie!*

Fore Street

INTRODUCTION

Maine is lobster and so much more. There's a lot going on here in terms of inventive eats and eateries, and it shows in the varied thousands of restaurants and specialty food shops that call Maine home. From the busy beach towns of the southern coast to the cool, mountainous forests and fields in the northwoods, there's a lot of variety and quality to explore in the largest of the New England states.

I've written about Maine eateries for the past 12 years in four books on New England cuisine and numerous articles for *Yankee* magazine. The state holds a special place in my culinary heart, and I consider myself fortunate to be tasked with writing this one.

As with my previous book in this series, *Unique Eats and Eateries of Connecticut*, I've focused on places that I consider to be organically unique—that is, restaurants and food shops that are not the creation of marketing firms or restaurant groups. Rather, the establishments contained herein are, for the most part, tried-and-true, mom-and-pop places that have been making good to great food for years, even decades. These places most truly reflect the unique culinary culture of the state.

The restaurants and specialty food shops included are just a sampling of what Maine has to offer and are by no means a comprehensive collection of the state's unique eateries nor a collection of the best. They're presented in no particular order, jumping around geographically to encourage browsing, in the hope that readers will find at least a few places they've never experienced before. Should you wish to explore any particular part of the state, there's a geographical appendix in the back of the book.

One of life's great joys is dining out, and it's my hope that you find this book informative, entertaining, and a useful guide to the many wonderful gustatory experiences to be had in the Pine Tree State.

Bon appétit!

Lakeshore House

UNIQUE EATS AND EATERIES OF MAINE

BOB'S CLAM HUT

A wonderful introduction to the great state of Maine

Serving as Maine's unofficial welcome wagon, Bob's Clam Hut sits on busy Route 1 just a mile or so from the state's southern border. Since its founding in 1956, Bob's has fed millions of hungry locals and curious travelers, many of them repeat customers who just can't seem to get enough of the clam shack's addictive deep-fried seafood.

Bob's story began when local youth Robert Kraft Sr. (not the same Robert Kraft who owns the New England Patriots football team) started frying up clams in his family's front yard and selling them to passing motorists on Route 1 right around the time the Maine Turnpike (I-95) was being built. With frequent traffic jams on the road, young Bob had a captive audience, and he perfected his fried clam recipe using clams he harvested from the local clam beds.

Kraft built a modest shack nearby, and Bob's remained pretty much the same until 1986 when local musician Mike Lundgarten bought Bob's and began a slow, steady expansion of the shack's physical space while honoring Kraft's original recipes for fried clams and more. An enclosed dining room was added, and Bob's became a year-round eatery while expanding the menu in bits and pieces.

Though Lundgarten recently sold Bob's to new owners, his stamp on the shack is indelible. Perhaps his greatest legacy is the hiring of Lillian Mango in the mid-1980s. A charming, opinionated local, Lillian took customer orders at the counter for more than 30 years, and she shared her unique method of breading and frying clams. You may order clams cooked Bob's original way, or you may get the "Lillian's Special," which calls for the clams to get an egg washing before breading and frying. For the best of both

Top left: Bob's year-round dining room.
Above left: A carton of Bob's amazing clam strips.
Top center: Bob's, as seen from busy US Route 1.
Above center: Digging for clams. Courtesy Bob's Clam Hut
Right: The "Clams 2 Ways" platter with sweet potato fries.

worlds, order the "Clams 2 Ways," a generous platter that features equal portions of Bob's and Lillian's crispy, crunchy fried bivalves.

Among other treats on Bob's menu are a generously portioned lobster roll, hearty homemade clam chowder made fresh daily, and excellent thin, crispy onion rings. There are some 10 deep-fryer units in the crowded kitchen, guaranteeing your deep-fried feast will be prepared quickly and served piping hot.

A small army of summer workers keep parking easy and smooth during peak time, directing traffic in and out of Bob's lot, eliminating any need for worry over how to ditch the car and get to the good stuff.

315 Route 1, Kittery, 207-439-4233
Bobsclamhut.com

If shopping is your thing, Bob's is surrounded by a string of outlet malls and stores lining Route 1, offering endless places to scratch your shopping itch and spend your hard-earned dollars.

MELBY'S MARKET AND EATERY

A hidden gem in bison country

Yellow paint is peeling from the building's three-story façade. A disused gas pump with a cracked-glass display sits out front. Strings of old Christmas lights dangle from the second-floor balcony over the front door. Parking is across the street in a dirt lot. Nobody would blame you for not stopping for a meal or a snack or some groceries. But that would be a mistake.

Equal parts restaurant and general store, Melby's is locally famous and has built quite a large following among travelers and seasonal residents savvy enough to cross the threshold and explore all that's offered within. And it's a year-round destination, with visitors arriving by car and pickup truck in the summer and by snowmobile in deepest winter.

There's been a general store in this building since the 1800s, and at some point, it began serving hot food under the name "Tut's General Store." In 1990, Tut's owners sold to Paul and Kay Legare, who changed the name to "Melby's Market and Eats," ramped up the menu, and built a loyal following from 1990 to 2016 before deciding to sell and take off in their camper to see North America. Current owners Wayne and Tracie Hill stepped into the breach, initially keeping the menu the same before putting their own wonderfully unique stamp on the eatery's offerings.

Inside the front door are racks of foodstuffs and coolers with soft drinks and beer, along with Melby's sweatshirts and hats for loyal customers to purchase. Then there's the order counter separating the groceries from the dining area with its tables and lengthy counter.

Left: Melby's is equal parts general store and restaurant.

Center: The modest dining room.

Top right: The renowned bison burger, locally sourced.

Above right: Melby's shabby exterior belies the treasures within.

Behold the whiteboards by the order counter, as they're a constantly changing display of such daily specials as ginger lime teriyaki stir-fry, rigatoni Genovese, swine sliders (pulled pork), and Happy Happy Joy Joy (a fried haddock sandwich served on Fridays).

Then there's the whiteboard listing some 50 sauces, primarily used with chicken wings but also serving as sandwich toppings and dippers for french fries. And the pièce de résistance is Melby's bison burger, made with bison meat from the Beech Hill Farm and Bison Ranch a mile and a half up the road.

The linoleum-floored dining room is a chatty area filled with good cheer and lots of talk between tables, counters, and waitstaff. Feel free to wander around and take in the humorous wall art while waiting for your meal to arrive.

Don't miss this roadside gem if you happen to be in the Waterford area. It's destined to put a smile on your face and some great food in your belly.

927 Valley Rd., Waterford, 207-583-4447
facebook.com/melbysmarketandeatery

CAFÉ THIS WAY

A breath of fresh air in tourist-crazy Bar Harbor

Should you find yourself on the streets of downtown Bar Harbor during the chaotic summer season feeling overwhelmed by the crowds of shoppers and sightseers, find your way to Café This Way, a quiet oasis just a half block off Main Street.

This wonderful spot is in a one-story shingled building tucked down an alley-like walkway off Mount Desert Street. For starters, there's an inviting outdoor patio with a bunch of umbrellaed tables and nicely tended flower boxes. Step within the café and you're treated to the visual splendor of a beautiful, open-floor-plan dining room, which has been divided into several separate areas, each featuring vivid paintings by Maine artist Neiley Harris and shelves of books built into the walls.

Then check out the tables, the tops of which sport whimsical illustrations (many also by Harris). A swirling sculpture-like art piece hangs suspended over the main part of the dining area, tastefully illuminated by track lighting. Chances are you'll be utterly charmed before even taking a seat.

Café This Way was cofounded and is owned by three women: Susanne Hathaway, Julie Harris (sister-in-law of the artist in residence), and Julie Berberian. They initially opened their doors in 1997. Two were recent graduates of nearby College of the Atlantic, and the third was cooking at a Bar Harbor restaurant that was about to close. Over coffee in the mid-1990s, the three decided to go in together and purchase a recently shuttered business spot on Mount

Many of the gorgeous Neiley Harris paintings that grace the walls of the dining rooms are Maine-themed and available for purchase.

Top left: Kit's Burrito.

Above left: One of the colorfully decorated dining nooks.

Top center: This way to Café This Way.

Above center: This lovely painting graces the café's entryway.

Right: A great spot for a bookish chat.

Desert Street. With no solid plan in place, they worked out a menu and an interior space design that have stood the test of time.

They describe their café as a place that serves eclectic food in a casual setting. Breakfast is the only meal currently being served, but what a breakfast it is. Eggs factor into nearly every dish, though there is an egg-less and dairy-free tofu dish for vegans that's seasoned with tamari and accompanied by mushrooms, onions, peppers, and broccoli. Veggie sausage is also available.

Many of the other dishes shoot straight down the middle with eggs, sausage, bacon, cheese, home fries, and more in various combinations. You may also order a "create your own" scramble, choosing between a broad range of veg, cheeses, and Mexican ingredients like black beans and salsa. And for those looking to wrap it all up in one handy package, go for Kit's Burrito, a marvelous scramble wrapped in a flour tortilla and garnished with generous scoops of sour cream, guacamole, and salsa.

14 ½ Mount Desert St., Bar Harbor, 207-288-4483
cafethisway.com

A1 DINER

An old-school diner with new ideas on diner cuisine

Perched on stilts astride a bridge above a parking lot and a creek, the A1 Diner has survived, even thrived, through decades of change in the town of Gardiner. This classic Worcester diner car is a magnet for diner aficionados and for those craving A1's alluring mix of classic diner fare and gourmet cooking.

Shortly after the end of World War II, Gardiner resident Ed Heald ordered a Worcester diner car from the factory in Massachusetts, had it delivered to Gardiner, and placed on its stilts where it still stands today. Heald named the diner after himself (the name is still emblazoned on the diner's façade), and he set about feeding the workers who toiled in Gardiner's factories and mills, which often ran 24/7 during busy times. Heald sold to a man named Maurice Wakefield in 1952, who changed the name to Wakefield's, and the practice of feeding hungry workers continued.

A third owner and name change occurred in 1978 when Al "Gibby" Giberson and his wife, Elizabeth, bought the diner and named it Giberson's. Their son, Mike, worked in the diner as a teen, and he and his partner, Neil Anderson, bought out Mom and Dad in 1988, heralding the age of the A1 Diner, a run-of-the-mill name for what would become an extraordinary place.

Mike and Neil spruced up the diner's appearance inside and out while preserving virtually all of the eatery's original features. The A1 still has its original marble countertop, chrome stools and backsplashes, and blue-and-black ceramic tilework throughout. The push-letter board menus are still in place and kept up to date.

And while much of the menu remained mainstream diner fare (franks and beans, bacon and eggs, meatloaf sandwich, pancakes

Left: The fresh-ground burger, made with locally raised beef.

Above center: A1's healthy, appealing fish tacos plate.

Top center: Classic neon dresses up the counter backsplash.

Top right: A traditional plate of beans and franks.

Above right: The A1 Diner's unmistakably retro look and feel are the pride of downtown Gardiner.

and waffles), Giberson and Anderson began introducing exotic dishes, such as Greek salad with fried calamari, Syrian cod cakes, lamb with eggplant curry and jasmine rice, and much more. These new offerings were warmly welcomed by Gardiner's increasingly professional crowd, as the town transitioned from manufacturing to a more service-based economy.

Current owner Aaron Harris, who for many years cooked in A1's kitchen, has continued the tradition of offering basic diner cookery alongside more adventurous dishes. Brunch at the A1 offers such diverse dishes as Maine crab benedict, biscuits and gravy, pastrami and potato hash, and lemon ricotta pancakes. A1 continues to be one of the most unique and cherished eateries in the state.

3 Bridge St., Gardiner, 207-582-4804

The A1's grilled chicken and brussels sprout sandwich is a favorite of the wife of the local funeral director. Upon learning this, the A1 named it the "Undertaker's Wife Sandwich."

BET'S FISH FRY

Massive portions, super-fresh fish

If you're only going to offer one thing in the restaurant business, you'd better do it well. And Bet's Fish Fry of Boothbay does it better than just about everyone else. With a menu that features only a fried fish sandwich, fish in a dish (fried fish, no bun), and hand-cut french fries, Bet's Fish Fry is living proof that focus, focus, focus can lead to success, success, success.

Owner and founder Bet Finocciaro has poured her heart and soul into this tiny operation, and her approach and philosophy have been steadfast ever since she first opened in 1993. Starting out in a converted camper-trailer, Bet found a spot in Boothbay next to Alfred Lewis's general store and leased the space for 50 dollars a month. Lewis let Bet hook up to his water and electric lines, a fry-o-later was installed, and Bet was off and running. Local high school kids were commissioned to paint the trailer in an imaginative way of their choosing.

Coming from a longtime Maine fishing family, Bet's first source of fish came from her family's boat, captained and crewed by her father and brother. From the get-go, Bet served local haddock fillets from the family's catch. She offered huge portions at very affordable prices, a practice that continues to this day. The fries come from Maine potatoes, cut fresh daily by Bet's crew.

The original trailer took a hit around the turn of the century when a car plowed into it, and Bet replaced it with a bigger, better trailer, which was also decorated by local high schoolers. (The

Bet's slogan, painted on the front of the shack, reads "FREE BEER TOMORROW."

Top left: Some of the creative yard art.

Above center: Bet's distinctive shack.

Above left: The simple, spare menu, painted on the side of the shack.

Top center: Bet's over-the-top fried haddock.

Right: Some of the shack's art, created by high school students.

second trailer has been replaced by a brightly painted, galvanized-roof shack.) You can't miss Bet's when driving into town. It's the most colorful sight on Route 27. She eventually purchased her small plot of land along with Lewis's general store building, giving her a more permanent foothold.

Today, Bet's fish comes from a couple of local suppliers who bring fresh-caught haddock daily. There's no fish left at the end of the day, thanks to Bet's exacting inventory control. The haddock is nicely breaded, cooked in clean oil, and then served up with (or without) bun and fries. Homemade tartar sauce and a dill lemon sauce are available, as is malt vinegar for those seeking a true fish-and-chips experience.

The tender flakiness and flavor of the fish keeps customers coming back time and again. The hours are limited (11 a.m. to 3 p.m., five days a week, in season), the seating is all outdoors, and the fried fish experience is divine.

Route 27, off the town square; Boothbay

LE MU EATS

A phenomenal restaurant in verdant Bethel

"Le mu noi" is a term of endearment in Laotian that means "the little pig." It's a moniker that chef/owner Sayvepen Sengsavang was given as a child. He has worn it proudly ever since, dropping the "noi" as he grew older, and he's incorporated it into the name of his marvelous restaurant on Main Street in Bethel.

The son of Laotian refugee immigrants, "Chef Sav," as he's known to family, friends, and coworkers, grew up in Virginia on a steady diet of Laotian and Southern cooking. This blend of cuisines, along with his formal training at the Virginia Culinary Institute, helped him forge his own unique culinary identity, which he's bringing to fruition in Maine.

Sav and his wife, Elise, a Bethel native, moved to Maine several years ago, and Sav initially found work as a cook at Norway Brewing Company. In 2018, the couple opened a blue-hued takeout stand, Le Mu Eats, on Mechanic Street in Bethel, with a walk-up order window and a spare menu posted next to it. People started taking notice almost immediately.

Plans were well underway for a second eatery, Mu Noi Eats, in Auburn when the pandemic hit, and after a year or so, the couple decided to shutter Mu Noi in its infancy and open a full-service version of Le Mu Eats. They found a spot in a lovely Main Street Bethel building that used to house longstanding bakery DiCocoa's Bakery and Café.

Le Mu Eats is lovely inside and out. A lengthy counter with stools provides diners with a full view of the chef and his associates in action, and it's a lively show. There are several tables of varying sizes scattered around the picture windows and a lovely patio overlooking Main Street for warm-weather dining.

Top left: Le Mu Eats, from the outside.

Above left: Chef Sav in his element.

Top center: A couple of dishes being prepped in the kitchen.

Above center: Nam khao.

Right: Fresh flowers sit atop the epoxied-chopsticks counter.

Now open for well over a year, Le Mu Eats has become a regional sensation. Some of the core dishes that helped make the takeout stand so popular remain on the menu at the new location. The Angry Rooster is a red-curry, buttermilk-brined chicken breast sandwich served with cabbage slaw and house pickles. There's a "Porke-Bowl," a poke-type creation with lemongrass pork at the core, and a very popular bahn mi sandwich. Thin, fresh hand-cut fries from local potatoes come in a variety of forms, both as sides and main dishes.

The menu changes constantly, based on what comes in from local fields and farms, so bring an open mind and a curious palate. Chef Sav and his crew are guaranteed to send you on your way smiling.

119 Main St., Bethel, 207-824-1155

The surface of the lengthy customer counter facing the kitchen is made from thousands of epoxied chopsticks.

THE CLAM SHACK

Serving what may be the world's best lobster roll

No summertime visit to the Kennebunks is complete without a stop at the legendary Clam Shack, Steve Kingston's seafood eatery next to the bridge connecting Kennebunk with neighboring Kennebunkport. The tiny, whitewashed shack churns out thousands of meals every week in peak season, and its lobster roll has gained well-deserved international fame through word-of-mouth, numerous awards, and much-deserved media attention.

The Clam Shack began its life as the offshoot of a Kennebunk seafood market. A man named Richard Jacques bought the market in 1968 and added a seafood shack to the side of the building by the bridge over the Kennebunk River. He began frying up local fish, clams, and scallops and served lobster rolls on unorthodox hamburger-style buns, breaking rank with most of the rest of New England's top-split hot dog bun approach.

Some 30 years later, Kingston, a local ice cream shop owner and entrepreneur, was driving by the shack on a snowy winter day with his wife when they noticed a FOR SALE sign tacked to the front. They inquired, outbid all other interested parties, and became the new owners. Steve stuck with the shack's menu, slowly modifying it over the years but for the most part sticking close to the spirit and purpose of the place.

Today, the Clam Shack boasts long lines of customers at their order window from Mother's Day through Columbus Day, most clamoring for the famous lobster roll as well as Steve's signature

The Clam Shack has been a longtime favorite of Kennebunkport's most famous citizens: the extended family of George H. W. Bush.

Left: A box of deep-fried clam strips.

Top center: The Clam Shack on a busy summer day.

Above center: The Clam Shack's famed lobster roll, flanked by fried clams and onion rings.

Right: The Clam Shack's owner Steve Kingston, tending the lobster cooker.

deep-fried seafood, clam and haddock chowders, and fresh-squeezed lemonade. (Beer and wine are also available.)

What makes Steve's lobster roll so unique? In addition to the bun, which is custom-baked at a nearby bakery, Kingston pays painstaking attention to the freshness of the lobster he serves. Buying exclusively from a few local fishermen, the lobsters are cooked in small batches and handpicked on the premises by a small army of summertime helpers. Each serving is portioned and placed in individual plastic containers, and then kept chilled on ice rather than refrigerated. The mayonnaise and butter that are served with each roll are locally sourced and of the highest quality. One bite into a Clam Shack lobster roll speaks volumes on why people travel from all over the country to try one.

There's still a small seafood market in the original building, but the shack is the focus of the fun here. The line may be long, but it moves quickly, a testament to the time, thought, and effort that the owner has put into making this little white shack the phenomenal success that it is.

2 Western Ave., Kennebunk, 207-967-3321
theclamshack.net

DOLLY'S RESTAURANT

One of the last vestiges of Acadian culinary culture in Northern Maine

Franco-American cuisine lives on in this charming casual restaurant overlooking the St. Joseph River and the Canadian bluffs on the opposite bank. Dolly's in Frenchville is about as north as one can go in Maine, and it's well worth the drive through potato-rich Aroostook County to experience this Acadian throwback.

Dolly's first opened its doors in the late 1980s, serving a combination of basic American fare along with French Canadian specialties. Odette Pelletier founded the restaurant and created the menu, which remains substantially the same today under the ownership of her son, Keith. The restaurant itself has the look and feel of a 1960s coffee shop—molded plastic booths, indoor/outdoor carpeting, and a jauntily slanted maroon ceiling with wooden beams. The atmosphere is cheery and chatty, and lots of natural light comes in through the picture windows lining the front of the restaurant. The servers are locals with many years on the job and deep relationships with regular customers.

The most important reason to seek this place out is its French-American cuisine, and that starts with ployes—pancake-like creations made with buckwheat batter and griddled on only one side, leaving dozens of pumice-like pock marks on the top. They're served in stacks of three and may be smothered in syrup, molasses,

Still hungry after your meal? Try a slice of one of the dozen-plus pies at Dolly's–everything from coconut to strawberry rhubarb and everything in between.

Top left: A plate of ployes.

Above left: Some of the art that adorns the walls at Dolly's.

Center: Dolly's decor is reminiscent of a 1960s rec room.

Right: Poutine with shaved steak.

or butter. They also come as a side dish with Dolly's famous Acadian chicken stew, a thick soup-like concoction. They may also be served with housemade cretons, a slathering of pork blended with spices that is reminiscent of liverwurst or pate.

Poutine is another popular French-Canadian dish here, and it comes in several forms. Starting with a base of french fries, thick, rich beef gravy is ladled over the top, and then finished off with a generous topping of chewy cheese curds. There's a tomato-based Italian version as well as a barbecue-sauce one, and shredded cheddar cheese may be substituted for curds. Meat in the form of shaved steak or ground beef are other add-ons. A small-size order of poutine is a meal in itself, so be judicious in your ordering.

Most of the rest of the menu hews toward standard American fare (burgers, steaks, some interesting seafood choices, and a dizzying array of sandwiches). But the real reason to come here is to partake of the Franco-American delights that represent a culinary handshake across the river border with the friendly Canadians on the other side.

17 US 1, Frenchville, 207-728-7050

THE GOLDENROD

The pride and joy of York Beach

Perfectly positioned to capture the appetites and imaginations of the thronging visitors to York Beach in summertime, the Goldenrod restaurant and confectionary has provided meals and treats to generations of Mainers and visitors from away since 1896. This seaside institution is particularly known for its "Goldenrod Kisses," saltwater taffy made fresh daily and in full view through the restaurant's picture windows.

Edward and Mattie Talpey seemed to anticipate York Beach's popularity in the late 1800s, when they opened their shop. Soon thereafter the first electric trains from population centers to the south began stopping at the Goldenrod's front door. Edward would hand-pull the sticky, sweet taffy in the store's front window. Today, antique machinery pulls, stretches, and twists the taffy before it's shaped and put on a cutting/wrapping machine, also on display. This is truly a throwback in time, which continues to amaze all passersby and patrons of the restaurant and candy store within. The Goldenrod is currently owned by David Peck, whose mother was a co-owner for many years.

The Goldenrod is housed in a massive, white, wood-frame structure that lends an historical look and feel to York Beach's compact business district. Just inside the front door is an undulating taffy and candy counter with dozens of different sweet treats beckoning from glass cases. The taffy is most frequently purchased in one-pound boxes, and there are about a dozen different flavors.

Just across from the candy counter is a lengthy lunch counter with some 20 swiveling chairs and a young, attentive staff ready to serve up meals and ice cream treats to the hungry hordes. Beyond the

Left: One of the antique taffy-pulling machines in action.
Top center: The Goldenrod stands tall and proud in York Beach.
Above center: Grilled ham and cheese with a side of homemade soup.
Right: An ice-cream sundae at the soda fountain counter.

lunch counter is a large, dimly lit dining room with spacious tables and comfortable chairs for those seeking a more leisurely repast.

The menu at the Goldenrod features breakfast items (waffles and griddle cakes), omelets, and bacon-and-egg dishes that are served throughout the day. For lunch and dinner customers, homemade clam chowder and a soup of the day make for good openers, followed by a parade of sandwiches, including a hefty roast beef sandwich and an exquisite bacon, lettuce, and tomato.

It would be a sin not to have ice cream for dessert here, and it's available by the scoop in a cup or on a cone or in beautifully constructed sundaes and splits.

Don't miss this throwback restaurant and sweets palace just a short walk from York's town beach. It's a sweet and dreamy culinary walk down memory lane.

2 Railroad Ave., York Beach, 207-363-2621
thegoldenrod.com

The Goldenrod still uses the same saltwater taffy recipe created and perfected by owner and founder Edward Talpey in the late 1800s.

PIZZA BY ALEX

Unique pizza with a loyal following

The town of Biddeford is rapidly developing a reputation as the latest foodie hotspot in Maine, with new restaurants popping up (especially in the old mill buildings along the Saco River) and savvy restaurateurs retrofitting new eateries into classic spots (think Palace Diner). Yet in downtown Biddeford, one restaurant has stood the test of time and changed nary a bit in over 60 years: Pizza by Alex.

Located in a two-story brick building with plate glass windows on the front and side and a large PIZZA BY ALEX neon sign hanging over the front door, this place is a throwback like no other. It's the kind of place one would typically walk by without giving any thought to checking out, but by all means, step inside. Pizza by Alex has been doing the same thing and doing it well, maintaining a grip on the imaginations and appetites of locals and bringing in seasonal travelers and residents year after year.

The pizzeria got its start in 1960 when Alex Mantis opened a small storefront pizzeria in downtown Biddeford and started serving his Greek-style, thin-crust pan pizza to curious customers. The pizza, made in countertop ovens, was a hit from the get-go, and within a few years Mantis moved to the larger quarters where the restaurant is currently located. The wood-paneled dining room was eventually expanded into the building next door, and both look strikingly similar to their original 1960s design with simple tables and wooden wing chairs facing the long order counter.

Pizza by Alex serves only one food in one size: pizza, which comes 10 inches in diameter with a variety of toppings. The pizzas are made fresh daily on the premises and are topped with cheddar cheese. All the standard toppings found in any pizzeria

Left: Pizza by Alex's famed neon sign over Alfred Street.
Top center: The newish countertop oven.
Above center: Pizza By Alex back in the day. Courtesy Pizza By Alex
Right: A pepperoni pizza, one of Alex's bestsellers.

are available, along with such specialties as kalamata olives, feta cheese, and anchovies, all nods to Alex's Greek heritage. Alex's Special pizza comes with onions, green peppers, salami, pepperoni, mushrooms, and Greek olives. Yaya's [sic] Greek pizza features onions, feta cheese, and spinach. (*YiaYia* means "grandmother" in Greek.)

The restaurant does a brisk trade in carryout, with each pizza sandwiched between two paper plates and slipped into a plain, brown paper bag. Many regular customers insist that their pizzas be cooked in the "old" (original) ovens as opposed to the newer conveyor belt ones, but you'd be hard-pressed to tell the difference.

Alex's nephew Andy has taken over the business, and the pizzeria's course for the future remains full steam ahead, much to the relief of die-hard customers.

93 Alfred St., Biddeford, 207-283-0002
pizzabyalexmaine.com

RUTH AND WIMPY'S

Lobster served with a side of humor

When driving east on Route 1 through Hancock in Downeast Maine, it's hard to miss the 11-foot fiberglass roadside lobster sculpture that marks the location of Ruth and Wimpy's restaurant. "Wilbur," as the red crustacean is known, has been beckoning travelers to stop in for lobster and much more at this true mom-and-pop place for more than three decades.

Ruth and Wimpy's is the brainchild of Ruth and Thurston (Wimpy) Wilbur, who purchased the roadside lobster joint in 1990 after Wimpy retired from 20 years as a long-haul trucker. Ruth is a native of Hancock, and Wimpy was raised in nearby Waltham. In short order, they started putting their unique stamp on the place, transforming it into a destination restaurant, thanks to lots of creative cookery, innovative dining room decor, and positive word-of-mouth.

Lobster is, of course, the main item on the menu—in fact, Ruth and Wimpy's serves it in more than 30 different ways. All the lobsters are cooked in open-air, wood-fired vats, a method commonly practiced at many lobster joints in and around Acadia. Most of the lobsters come from Sorrento Lobster in the nearby town of the same name. On a busy summer day, more than 150 pounds of fresh lobster meat will be handpicked at Ruth and Wimpy's for use in its many lobster offerings.

Over the years, the couple has expanded the menu to more than 100 different dishes, many of them seafood-based, along with

Among the more than 30 ways Ruth and Wimpy's serves lobster: lobster salad, lobster stew, lobster roll, lobster fondue, lobster chowder, lobster bisque, lobster scampi, and, of course, whole boiled lobster.

Top left: Lobsters and clams emerging from Ruth and Wimpy's outdoor cookers.

Above left: Wilbur the lobster.

Top right: Ruth and Wimpy's whimsical roadside sign.

Above right: Ruth and Wimpy Wilbur.

dozens of others ranging from pasta and steaks to barbecue and home-baked pie. There are 10 different types of burgers alone. The eatery's somewhat cramped kitchen is a beehive of activity from early morning onward, with Ruth at the helm. (Wimpy is more likely to be found in the lobster-picking shed adjacent to the restaurant, where he can sit at his open-air window and converse with curious customers while he gets the lobster meat ready for dozens of meals.)

The restaurant's interior is a reflection of many of Wimpy's passions and hobbies. An avid collector, one room is lined with shelves containing dozens of Wimpy's die-cast model cars while another displays beer bottles from seemingly everywhere. Outside, there's a covered, open-air dining room as well as picnic tables and Adirondack chairs for sitting in while waiting for a table or digesting after a large repast.

Custom car owners congregate at Ruth and Wimpy's almost nightly in the summertime. Feel free to stroll around and check out the wheels before or after your meal.

792 US Highway 1, Hancock, 207-422-3723
ruthandwimpys.com

BRUNSWICK DINER

A favorite among students, townies, and passersby

The Brunswick Diner has had its fair share of changes and adaptations over the years, yet it carries on admirably and has settled into its golden age under the loving ownership of Jane Davis, the diner's owner for the past 24 years. It stands like a red beacon on busy Pleasant Street, with its barrel roof and cubed-glass entryway.

One of the reasons for the diner's lasting appeal is its down-home cooking, with its strong roster of breakfast favorites and its lunchtime menu highlighted by dishes drawing heavily from the local seas. This compelling combination, when paired with great service and authentically retro decor, guarantees a steady stream of hungry, curious customers.

The diner debuted in Brunswick in 1946, after a brief life in Norway, Maine, where it was known as the Miss Norway Diner. It's had five different owners in Brunswick, including Ms. Davis.

Step into the diner today, and the first thing you notice is the refurbished, fully operational replica of a 1946 One More Time Wurlitzer jukebox. This gem sets the tone for the fun to be had. There's also about 30 coffee mugs suspended from the ceiling on hooks behind the counter, each one belonging to a regular customer.

The long counter with swiveling stools is a great place to grab a seat and watch the servers in action. As with many classic diners, the kitchen has been moved to a space in the back, but lucky folks on the center stools can peer into the kitchen through a window and watch the cooks work their magic on the diner's griddle. Also behind the counter is a lovely neon BRUNSWICK DINER clock.

Like all good diners, this is a neighborhood place, including lots of students from nearby Bowdoin College. Add the vacationers

Left: The Yard Omelet with all the trimmings.
Center: The diner's counter and colorful interior.
Right: Brunswick Diner's bright-red entryway.

who make this place a regular stop while motoring by, and the Brunswick can boast a steady, loyal customer base.

Breakfast is the main meal served, featuring egg sandwiches, eggs benedict dishes, omelets, and specialties such as the Bowdoin Bowl, a combination of tater tots, brussels sprouts, cheddar cheese, poached eggs, and hollandaise sauce.

Lunchtime items offer a couple of seasonal lobster dishes, including a popular lobster roll. Other nautical favorites include crab cakes and a Maine monkfish stew made with locally procured vegetables. The BD Burger comes with a ton of toppings and is a favorite with carnivores.

Stop in here for some great food and good vibes before heading back out on Route 1 for more Midcoast Maine adventures.

101 Pleasant St. (Route 1), Brunswick, 207-721-1134
brunswickdiner.com

The curiously named "Yard Omelet" refers to the hardworking boatyard at Bath Iron Works in Bath, Maine. The breakfast dish is popular with numerous yard workers who stop by for it before or after their shifts.

ELEVATION SUSHI AND TACOS

Something new, exciting (and unexpected) in Bridgton

East meets West meets South of the Border at this relatively new restaurant in the Western Maine town of Bridgton. The multiethnic eatery has been embraced by locals and visitors alike in its early goings, seen as a breath of fresh air on the local dining scene.

This cozy, elevated storefront restaurant offers a few different seating options within its relatively small interior. First, there's the sushi bar with several stools, offering bird's-eye views of the sushi chef at work and of the lovely, refrigerated slabs of fish used in their creations. Then there are several tables made from irregular pieces of lacquered wood and a wooden counter in the front window with high-top stools, presenting views of Main Street. In warmer months, an open-air front porch with a few tables is a great spot to enjoy a light and refreshing repast.

Elevation is the brainchild of Kimberley Morton and Mike Perez and their son-in-law, John Dexter. All three are relatively recent transplants from Southern California, who claim that missing the great Japanese and Mexican foods prevalent in the West inspired them to open a restaurant in Western Maine. Kimberley owned a restaurant in California years ago, and son-in-law, John, has worked as a sushi chef in Los Angeles and Las Vegas. Perez, recently retired from a long career in auto parts distribution, has trained under John and has fit in very nicely as John's sushi-prep person.

The menu leans more toward the world of sushi, with standard rolls such as spicy tuna, shrimp tempura, California, salmon in various configurations, and eel. Then there are Elevation's

Left: Some of the restaurant's lovely wall art.
Top center left: Elevation's snappy front entrance.
Above center left: Pork street tacos.
Center right: The cozy, intimate sushi bar.
Right: A spicy tuna roll and a California roll.

"Specialty" rolls: California Betty (a California roll topped with salmon, slices of lemon, garlic Ponzu, and green onion); the Main Street (lobster with asparagus, avocado, mixed greens, and garlic aioli); the Bridgton (spicy crab with cucumber and avocado, dressed with Ebi shrimp, avocado, jalapeno, eel sauce, spicy mayo, and sriracha); and about a dozen more of various configurations. Sashimi appetizers come in five varieties.

On the Mexican side of things, tacos lead with way with carne asada, chicken, pork, and vegetable versions as well as inventive sushi tacos (tuna poke with microgreens). These softshell beauties come with a choice of chips and salsa or Spanish rice on the side.

This is an ideal place to share your selections with fellow diners in your party, so all of you may partake of the myriad creative offerings from this refreshing new addition to the Bridgton dining scene.

103 Main St., Unit 1, Bridgton, 207-803-8752

Be sure to check out the wonderful wall murals of a grabby octopus and another of a flowering tree that grace Elevation's interior. They're the work of talented local artist Kate Erwin.

DUCKFAT

Great name, even better food

Looking every bit like a quaint European bistro with its beige, black, and tan awning and outdoor café seating in front, Duckfat has been a magnet for crowds of diners daily since it opened its doors on Portland's Middle Street in 2005. The brainchild of Nancy Pugh and Rob Evans, Duckfat's tender, crispy Belgian frites, served in paper cones, have become an iconic fixture on the Portland dining scene.

The idea for Duckfat took root in 2003 when Nancy surprised husband Rob with a trip for his 40th birthday to Amsterdam. There they encountered a Belgian frites stand and were instantly smitten; they began dreaming about bringing the unusual taste treat back to Portland. The two had purchased the famed restaurant Hugo's in 2000, and within a year Rob was garnering national acclaim as Hugo's chef. In 2005, a space opened up a block or so east on Middle Street. The couple bought it and launched their dream eatery later that year.

What makes Duckfat so unique? First and foremost, it's the frites, made using homegrown Maine Norwis potatoes from Green Thumb Farms in Fryeburg. The spuds are freshly cut each day, and then fried once in duck fat. Each order is then fried in duck fat again just prior to serving, guaranteeing the proper taste and crispiness that has become Duckfat's hallmark.

The frites are served in a paper cone and come with your choice of two to three dipping sauces, depending on the order size. Choose from truffle ketchup, Thai chili mayo, curry mayo, horseradish mayo, or garlic mayo. (All mayos are made on the premises.)

The frites also form the basis of another signature Duckfat specialty: poutine. A working-class French-Canadian dish, poutine consists of fried potatoes topped with cheese curds and gravy, a

Left: A cone of Duckfat's famed frites.

Top center: Duckfat's colorful entrance, reminiscent of a European bistro.

Above center: A plate of poutine with duck confit.

Right: Duckfat's tomato fennel soup.

stick-to-your-ribs meal that Duckfat customizes with its unique gravy made from roasted duck bones. Other menu highlights include cider-poached beets, cream of tomato fennel soup, and several types of grilled panini sandwiches.

Seating is limited, and reservations aren't taken, so try to visit during non-peak times, such as mid-afternoon. There are several cozy tables inside, along with a counter and five stools, providing a glimpse into the kitchen. Outdoor seating is available seasonally. Lots of folks simply order a cone of frites and take it to go for great snacking while exploring Portland's Old Port neighborhood.

Duckfat is certainly one of Portland's top food destinations, one that should be on any avid foodie's list.

43 Middle St., Portland, 207-774-8080
duckfat.com

Duckfat has a frites shack with an order window similar to the one that initially captivated the owners on their 2003 trip to Amsterdam. It's located nearby on Portland's Washington Street.

KEN'S PLACE

Authentic seafood with a pine forest backdrop

Pine Point Road in Scarborough winds its way toward Old Orchard Beach and its many seaside attractions. Along the road be sure to stop at Ken's Place, a seafood emporium that's been serving up great eats since 1927. And for the past 25 years or so, Ken's has been in the good hands of owner Dave Wilcox, who has elevated the dine-in-the-rough eatery to amazing heights.

Ken's takes its name from founder Ken Skillings, who started the seafood stand out of his garage nearly 100 years ago. He and a few of his buddies started digging clams out of the local flats, shucking them, frying them up or making them into clam cakes, and selling them to passing motorists. The original Ken's was in a different location on Pine Point Road, a little closer to the beach area and the large Snow's Clams processing plant.

Ken sold the business to the Bergeron family in 1963, and the Bergerons moved Ken's to its current location amidst a grove of pine trees. The gray painted shack was gussied up with indoor eating areas added to the front and sides. Numerous picnic tables were set up all around the property, including a bunch in the pine tree grove out back. This is pretty much the layout of Ken's today.

Wilcox, a food manager at a seafood place in Freeport, was shopping around for a restaurant to buy, and he snapped up Ken's when the Bergerons put it up for sale in the late 1990s. He then threw himself full bore into remodeling the interior, expanding the menu, and setting the blueprint for the great seafood shack it is today.

Ken's has five acres of grounds, much of it covered with shady pine trees and numerous picnic tables scattered about for forested outdoor dining.

Top left: A lobster dinner.

Above left: The picnic tables out front are a popular spot for a quick lunch or dinner.

Top center: Ken's sign pulls in beachgoers on their way to and from the Old Orchard and Pine Point beaches.

Above center: A plate of Ken's fish & chips, made with freshly filleted haddock.

Right: The shrimp and whole-belly clam combo platter.

Dave pays particularly close attention to procuring the freshest seafood he can find. Most of it is locally sourced, and he goes to great lengths to do everything right, even having all his lobster meat for rolls and stews picked fresh in the kitchen every day. This makes a huge difference in the flavor of his lobster dishes. Haddock is also filleted fresh daily in the kitchen.

In addition to all the excellent deep-fried seafood and fresh-picked lobster, there's a raw bar for oysters, clams, and boiled shrimp and a full bar for libations with your meal. Mother's Day is the busiest day at Ken's, when some 2,000 customers are typically served, many of them opting for the traditional clam cakes for which Ken's is famous.

This place is a great stop-off when traveling to or from Old Orchard Beach. Be sure to check it out when you're in the area.

207 Pine Point Rd., Scarborough, 207-883-6611

BECKY'S DINER

A steady beacon in food-crazy Portland

In 1991, the Portland waterfront was blessed with the opening of a new (and apparently much needed) restaurant aimed at feeding local fishermen and dock workers up and down Commercial Street. Becky's Diner was the brainchild of Portland resident Becky Rand, a recently divorced mother with six children who needed to provide for her young family. Since that opening, the waterfront eatery has been constantly busy, initially serving only breakfast, and then quickly expanding with lunch and dinner hours and offerings. Hard work has paid off for Rand and her family, and the local community supports them with hundreds of customers every day.

The diner began life as a modest, one-story, cinder-block building that had to fight for a zoning variance in order to set up shop on the busy commercial waterfront. Situated at the base of High Street, the diner was an instant hit with the wharf rats working the fishing boats and cargo ships docked literally in Becky's backyard.

The diner underwent a significant remodeling and expansion in 2007, adding a second floor that contains primarily large baking ovens and tables. (Becky's bakes all its own bread, cakes, cookies, pies, and more, and sells a wide variety of baked goods at the front counter.) The cedar-shingled exterior resembles a beach house more than the diner that it is. The center of the first-floor dining area consists of a long counter with some 20 stools flanked by numerous booths and tables along the walls. A tin ceiling adds to the cozy atmosphere.

Breakfast is the main meal of the day at Becky's, and it doesn't disappoint. High-quality victuals at reasonable prices keep customers coming back for more. There are standard plates of eggs,

Left: Becky's distinctive sign and entryway on Commercial Street.

Center: The Hobson's Wharf Special.

Top right: The famed roast turkey dinner.

Above right: Becky's brewed coffee—a great way to start the day.

bacon, sausage, corned beef hash, French toast, pancakes, and more. The Lobster Omelette brings a lot of Maine to the morning menu, with generous chunks of lobster meat and Swiss cheese. There are also excellent fruit bowls with yogurt and granola for the more healthful diners.

Seafood is prominently featured on the lunch and dinner menus with various haddock dishes and chowders and a killer lobster roll served with either mayo or drawn butter. A broad array of sandwiches and seafood platters are available late morning throughout the evening.

And don't forget the dinnertime diner fare—meatloaf, roast turkey dinner, and chopped sirloin patties smothered in beef gravy with mashed potatoes and fresh veg on the side.

Becky's now-grown kids play key roles in the restaurant's current success, making this place a true family treasure.

390 Commercial St., Portland, 207-773-7070
beckysdiner.com

SPRAGUE'S LOBSTER

Lobster rolls, lobster dinners, and much more

It can be quite challenging to thrive in the shadow of a Maine juggernaut like Red's Eats, but Sprague's Lobster has been doing that for more than 30 years—and with plenty of success.

Right across the street from Red's, Sprague's offers what many consider to be a welcome alternative to the madness that Red's can be on a hot summer day. With little or no lines and a lobster roll every bit as good as Red's, owner Frank Sprague has staked out his own wonderful identity on the Wiscasset waterfront.

Frank got his start in the lobster business back in the 1970s as a caterer, hauling around his two- by five-foot, wood-fired lobster boiler, setting it up for picnics, receptions, reunions, and more. He could cook as many as 100 lobsters at a time. Life on the road took its toll, so in 1988 he started renting a spot next to Wiscasset's town dock on the Sheepscot River.

Ten years later, the town built a bigger, better town dock right next to Route 1, and Sprague's moved to the location it currently occupies. With great views of the river (and of Red's across the road), Frank and his family have settled into a nice existence on the sunny dock.

Sprague's occupies a couple of the dock's several shacks. The first one you'll encounter is the fry shack, where all orders are placed. The other shack is where Frank and his crew boil up lobsters and bags of steamers. (Unlike Red's, you may get a whole lobster at Sprague's.) Numerous umbrellaed picnic tables are scattered on the dock, offering a comfortable place to dine along with splendid views of the river.

What's to eat here? Sprague's menu offers just about anything you'd expect to find at a Maine seafood shack. In addition to whole

Left: A whole-lobster dinner.

Top center: Sprague's storage shed, where live lobsters are kept.

Above center: Frank Sprague.

Top right: Sprague's meaty lobster roll.

Above right: Sprague's comfy deck and fry shack.

lobsters and lobster rolls, there's a popular crabmeat roll, filled with fresh-picked Maine crabmeat, mayo, and seasonings, all tucked into a toasted, split-top bun. The fried haddock is another popular seafood sandwich offering.

The deep fryers at Sprague's put forth clam cakes, clam fritters, fish & chips, and fresh, hand-cut french fries. There's also a milky chowder chock-full of clams, perfectly cooked potato cubes, and nicely seasoned broth prepared fresh daily by Frank.

Once you're set up with your victuals at one of the picnic tables, be thankful you're not still standing in line across the street.

22 Main St., Wiscasset, 207-882-1236

There's a clothesline with a cowbell stretching between the fry shack and lobster shack. Orders for whole lobster are attached by clothespin to the line and hoisted to the lobster shack for cooking.

BAGADUCE LUNCH

Maine seafood as it's meant to be

Quite a bit of backroad driving is required to get to Bagaduce Lunch on the Blue Hill peninsula, but it's worth every mile of scenery and charm—and the big payoff comes when you pull up in front of this classic Maine eatery.

Bagaduce (pronounced bag-uh-DOOS) sits astride the extremely tidal Bagaduce River, next to a two-lane bridge over the stream that courses back and forth with great force a couple of times a day. It's quite a sight to see bathers jump off one side of the low-slung bridge and then come shooting out the other side seconds later, propelled by the strong tidal pull. (Such activity is discouraged, by the way.) The lunch stand is a low-slung, whitewashed shack with red trim and a simple, black-and-white BAGADUCE LUNCH sign nailed to the roof.

The seafood shack opened in 1946 and has been in the same family ever since. The original shack was smaller than the current one, which was rebuilt and expanded in 2010, but the menu has remained pretty much the same for more than 75 years, featuring locally sourced seafood.

Sidney and Bernice Snow founded Bagaduce, and it's currently owned and run by the Snows' granddaughter, Judy, and her husband, Mike, who took over in 1997. Judy and her daughter operate the busy order and pickup windows on the shack's front, while Mike and a helper or two do all the prep work and cooking.

Bagaduce Lunch was honored in 2008 with a James Beard America's Classic award for being a truly unique American dining establishment. The medal from the foundation is proudly kept by the counter inside the shack.

Top left: The shack on the Bagaduce River.

Above left: The picnic peninsula out back.

Top center: Whole-belly fried clam basket.

Above center: Bagaduce's simple, colorful menu.

Right: The shack's James Beard America's Classic award.

The Bagaduce experience begins with stepping up to the order window and perusing the menu on the front of the building. The focus here is on fried seafood. There is a good lobster roll, but the fried clams are Bagaduce's pride and joy, along with their famous fried haddock sandwich and fried scallops, all of which come from local sources. The tartar sauce, coleslaw, and three-bean salad are homemade, as are home-baked pies served up by the slice for dessert. Maine's Gifford Ice Cream has been on the menu here for years.

Dining at Bagaduce is a great outdoor experience. Some 25 picnic tables are scattered around the grounds next to and in back of the shack, several of which are positioned on a short peninsula jutting out into the broad, tidal river. An American flag flaps in the breeze at the end of the peninsula, where boaters often pull up and dock for a meal. Bald eagles often make appearances during the shack's short season from Memorial Day through Labor Day. This iconoclastic shack is well worth the out-of-the-way drive.

145 Frank's Flat Rd., Penobscot, 207-326-4197

SIMONES' HOT DOG STAND

Serving up "red snappers" for more than 100 years

If you've been in the restaurant business for 115 years (and counting), you must be doing something right. In the case of Simones' Hot Dog Stand in Lewiston, it's a combination of good food, great service, and a wonderful community atmosphere.

Simones' (pronounced Sih-MOAN-ace) first opened its doors in downtown Lewiston in 1908, when the mills along the Androscoggin River were going strong and thousands of workers, many of them recent immigrants, needed a place to get a quick, cheap meal. Greek immigrant James Simones and his brother decided to open a small eatery offering one item only: hot dogs. They served up a unique type of wiener, the "red snapper," so-called because of the natural red dye that gave the dogs a glowing crimson appearance, and the snapping sound that occurred when the dogs were bitten into.

The original stand had four stools (eventually expanded to eight) and no tables and was located on Park Alley until 1966, when Simones' moved across the street to a larger space with a counter, a couple of small rooms, and several tables. Snappers were (and are) the main draw on the menu, though breakfast items and sandwiches like burgers and subs have been added over the years.

Current owner Jimmy Simones has been working at the eatery since the early 1970s, along with wife Linda, and their children have grown into the business. It's a real family affair with a strong community following. Some customers have been coming for more than 30 years; all they have to do is pull into the parking lot and the Simones's already know what to prepare for them.

The restaurant's interior is fittingly colored bright red and yellow, reminiscent of hot dogs tricked out with mustard. The

Left: A Simones' sign from days gone by.

Top center: Simones' distinctive red brick building.

Above center: A couple of red snappers.

Top right: The Super Omelet, with the works.

Above right: One of the hot dog stand's colorful dining rooms.

standard order for a hot dog is the "loaded"—with onions, mustard, and relish. There's also a great kraut dog as well as a chili dog smothered in homemade chili sauce. The hot dogs and buns are steamed to a perfect temperature and texture, and two dogs is the minimum recommended order.

The breakfast menu, which has expanded steadily over the years, has some great omelets and other griddle specialties. Of particular note is the "Georgey," an egg, cheese, and meat breakfast sandwich served on a grilled English muffin. It's named after the owner's son, who is in turn named after Jimmy's father.

Though downtown Lewiston has seen many changes over the years, Simones' remains a model of consistency and loving hospitality to its citizens, who keep coming back.

99 Chestnut St., Lewiston
207-782-8431

If you want to be considered a regular at Simones', order "two loaded" hot dogs with a "dirty cow" (chocolate milk) to wash them down.

BITE INTO MAINE

What a lobster roll food truck should be

What are the odds that a married couple from the Midwest would become major players in Maine's highly competitive lobster roll scene—and virtually overnight? It happened a little over 10 years ago, when a Minnesota couple's Bite Into Maine food truck rolled into a Cape Elizabeth park and hung out its menu.

Karl and Sarah Sutton were graphic artists in the Gopher State when they decided to relocate to Portland in the mid-2000s. They became big fans of lobster rolls, a taste treat not easily found back in their homeland. Thinking it might be fun to have a food truck serving lobster rolls around the Portland area, they applied for a permit to set up a stand in Fort Williams Park, home of the world-famous Portland Head Light lighthouse. Much to their shock, they won the permit and started shopping around for a utility trailer. (Motorized food trucks aren't allowed in the park.) The agreement with the park calls for driving the trailer in every morning during summer, setting up shop, and driving the trailer out at the end of the day.

Space is tight in the trailer, but the design-oriented Suttons have optimized every square inch. Food prep is done at their commissary in nearby Scarborough, and light cooking and assembly is done while set up in the park. The amount and variety of foods and snacks served up from the diminutive trailer is quite amazing.

Bite Into Maine serves up six types of lobster rolls: a Maine-style roll dressed in mayonnaise and chives; a Connecticut roll with warmed lobster and melted butter; the Picnic-style Roll, which features coleslaw, lobster meat, celery salt, and butter; and finally, three more cold rolls variously seasoned with just the

Top left: The "truck" in Fort Williams Park.

Above left: The Picnic-style Roll.

Top center: The Maine-style Roll.

Above center: Portland Head Light.

Right: Owners Sarah and Karl Sutton.

right amounts of wasabi, curry, or chipotle. All rolls are served on buttered, toasted, split-top hot dog buns.

Local Maine-made sodas, including Moxie Soda, are available.

One more thing working in favor of Bite Into Maine: it sits on a rise that overlooks Portland Head Light, one of the most beautiful and recognizable lighthouses in America. The view of the lighthouse with the sea as a backdrop is as gorgeous as it sounds. You're welcome to walk the grounds and take in the salty air wafting off the ocean. Not a bad way to spend a summer day!

1000 Shore Rd., Cape Elizabeth, 207-289-6142
biteintomaine.com

Can't make it out to Fort Williams Park? Feel free to visit Bite Into Maine's commissary in Scarborough or their trailer at famed Allagash Brewery in Portland.

FORE STREET

The restaurant that always seems to get it right

Fore Street embodies everything that's great about Portland restaurants: historic setting, outstanding innovative food, smart, attentive service—a real world-class experience from beginning to end.

Start with the history. Fore Street is housed in a solidly constructed brick warehouse building of yore with large, paned windows in all the dining areas front, side, and back, letting in lots of natural light. It sits in the Old Port neighborhood, the historic, beating heart of the city.

Then there's the layout of the restaurant. It's an open floor plan with a couple of levels of tables overlooking a totally open kitchen. Bustling with white-aproned chefs working in perfect unison on a multitude of tasks, the food-prep floor show includes grilling meats on an open turnspit to baking native mussels in cast-iron skillets shoved into a wood-burning oven to chopping fresh veg and shucking fresh oysters taken from the large glassed-in crisper/chiller.

Back in 1996, local Maine chef Sam Hayward, who recently closed his small restaurant in Brunswick, launched a far more ambitious project featuring wood-hearth cooking and farm-to-fork fresh vegetables and seafood procured from a select group of local farmers and fishermen. Coming across the warehouse space and sketching out his plans for a unique brick hearth oven, wood-smoke grill, and old-fashioned turnspit roaster, Fore Street started to come into focus.

The end result is a culinary gem that has treated three decades of diners to the most extraordinary and exceptional cooking that food-mad Portland has ever experienced. Much of this success is due to the consistently fine staff and suppliers that Fore Street has hired and kept, many for years on end, creating a consistently high level of fine food and attentive service.

Left: Fore Street's exquisitely appointed dining room, overlooking the open kitchen.

Top center: Fore Street's amazing open kitchen is a beehive of activity.

Above center: The famed roasted, marinated half chicken.

Right: A basket of fresh baked bread from Standard Baking Co.

In addition to the ringside dining room, there's a convivial bar area in the front of the building with a dozen or so stools and several tables along the front windows. It's a great place to sip, to dine, and to make new friends.

The menu changes daily, but some regular items not to miss are the wood-oven roasted Maine mussels, the wood-grilled hangar steak, and the turnspit roasted dry rubbed pork loin or the roasted, marinated half chicken.

There's dinner service only, and reservations are strongly recommended, though Fore Street leaves open several tables and the bar area for walk-ins each night. Don't miss this top-line Portland dining experience.

288 Fore St., Portland, 207-775-2717
forestreet.biz

Like top-shelf baked goods? Check out Standard Baking Co., Fore Street's partner and neighbor one floor down, with a separate entrance on the building's backside. Many consider Standard to be the best bakery in the city.

ROUND POND LOBSTER

Simple pleasures are the best

"Go where the locals go" is a good rule of thumb any time you're seeking a place to dine. This certainly is the case when inquiring about where to go for a lobster dinner on Maine's Pemaquid peninsula. Round Pond Lobster in the tiny village of Round Pond has for many years been the go-to place for locals and a popular spot for frequent visitors who know a good thing when they've found it.

Round Pond Lobster has roots going back decades that are inextricably tied to the local lobster industry. Current proprietor Edward "Buddy" Poland traces at least a couple generations of his family back to the wharf that Round Pond calls home. A lobstering family in the area since the 1930s, Buddy's father purchased the wharf in 1962 for $600. Buddy's grandfather thought his son had overpaid. The wharf was expanded to its current size in 1989, and it's been a going concern in the Poland family ever since.

The wharf has served as a base of operations for many lobstermen over the years, with Buddy and his forebears selling bait and traps to local lobstermen, who then bring their catch to the wharf where it's purchased by the Polands and shipped inland to various locations and to Canada for processing.

Buddy served in the navy from 1977 to 1981, and upon his return to Round Pond, he agreed to work temporarily on the wharf beside his father and brothers while an ad was run in the local paper for a permanent employee. Long story short, Buddy's still there, running the operation with the help of his daughter, Clara, and one or two others. "As far as I know that help-wanted ad is still running," Buddy quips in his distinctive Maine accent.

In 1986, the Polands started cooking up and serving some of their catch for people to enjoy on the dock. They set up several picnic

Top left: Clara Poland, Buddy's daughter and longtime helper.

Above left: Round Pond's dining deck on the pier.

Top center: Lobster, corn, and butter.

Top right: Round Pond's owner Buddy Poland.

Above right: Round Pond Lobster's modest digs.

tables, and customers started showing up. That tradition, which runs from Father's Day through Labor Day, thankfully still continues.

The menu is simple and spare: whole boiled lobsters, steamers, corn on the cob, and potato chips. There's a soda machine next to the modest shack, and people may bring their own alcoholic beverages, side dishes, and desserts. The sheer simplicity of the place, along with Buddy's longstanding reputation as a colorful character and gracious host, has made Round Pond Lobster a legend in Midcoast Maine. It should be at the top of your list of places to consider for an authentic lobster dinner.

25 Landing Rd., Round Pond, 207-529-5725

THIRD ALARM DINER

Great food and drink in a shrine to firefighters

Located in a little red box of a building attached to a frame house in downtown Sanford, Third Alarm Diner pays tribute to firefighters past and present in this old Southern Maine mill town. Inside and out, firefighting is the theme, yet it's the food, the drink, and the friendly atmosphere that make this place a Southern Maine standout.

The diner has been around for an untold number of years, initially serving the hundreds of workers in the local mills along the Mousam River, which runs through town. There's still a brick mill building just across the street from the diner, along with several others scattered around town. It was originally called Currier's Diner until a couple of local firemen purchased it and gave it the firefighter's name and theme that it bears to this day.

Step inside and you'll come face-to-face with a heavy, flame-retardant firefighter's jacket in a glass display case, along with firefighter shirts, helmets, hoses, nozzles, and old alarm boxes. The walls bear photos showing local firefighters in action over the years. And if you step outside and check out the side of the building, there's a mural depicting a hook-and-ladder and firefighters in action.

Wendy Fawcett has owned Third Alarm since 2019. Before that, she waitressed at the diner for 10 years, making many friends and engendering loyal customers who keep coming back for the good food and warm camaraderie. It's truly a meeting place for everyone in town, and some customers have been coming here for decades.

Wendy made some key changes when she took ownership. First, breakfast is now served all day, even during the dinner hours, an increasing rarity in restaurants these days. You may also get some lunch and dinner items in the morning, such as fried clams, if you're so inclined.

Left: Eggs Benedict, served all day.

Top center: The firefighter mural on the outside wall.

Above center: Third Alarm Diner, open for business.

Right: The Smokehouse Burger.

Fawcett has focused the menu on Third Alarm's great selection of grilled burgers (10 different types), half a dozen different types of melts, and deep-fried seafood. At breakfast, omelets and eggs benedict dishes (10 and five types, respectively) give hungry customers plenty to choose from.

Perhaps the biggest change (and one of the most welcome) is the serving of alcohol. This has proven popular with customers any time of day. Not many other diners offer flights of margaritas and mimosas (select four flavors of each).

47 Washington St., Sanford, 207-490-0557
thirdalarmdiner.com

Thirsty? Try the Third Alarm Rum Bucket (a special blend of rums) or the Bloody Mary Bucket. Both are served in small plastic facsimiles of old-fashioned fire buckets.

ROLLING FATTIES

An Airstream trailer begets a great eatery with a funny name

With a name like Rolling Fatties, it's pretty easy to get folks curious to learn more about this unusual eatery. It's a nice tease that serves as an entree to an excellent food-and-drink experience in the four-season wonderland that is Central Maine's Carrabassett Valley.

"Fatties," as it's known to locals, began life as a food truck some 10 years ago. Founders and owners Pat and Rob MacMichael met years earlier while working at a restaurant. They eventually married and settled into divergent careers for several years before deciding they'd like to launch a business in order to spend more time together. They thought serving food consisting of local ingredients would be fun and rewarding, and the quickest and cheapest way to begin was to get a food truck.

The MacMichaels purchased a 1970s Airstream trailer and completely renovated and retrofitted it with a tiny kitchen and a couple of order/pickup windows. They created the menu themselves, with a big, fat burrito being the centerpiece of their offerings. They made (and still make) their tortillas from scratch. The pudgy burritos are packed with beans and groat (a local oat grain with the husk removed, a stand-in for rice). In addition, several meat items may be added to your fattie, such as steak, burger, pork, or chicken, all locally grown. Nonmeat additions include house-pickled jalapenos, locally sourced ricotta cheese, Monterey Jack cheese from Cabot in Vermont, and several different types of salsas.

Top left: Fatties's outdoor bar and summer dining area.

Above left: The duo-toned orange frame building housing Fatties's kitchen, bar, and wintertime dining rooms.

Center: The famed Fatties's burrito, packed with meat, beans, and groat.

Right: The fun at Rolling Fatties begins here.

If you want to roll the dice on one of Fatties's custom burritos, try the Freedom Fatty, a burrito stuffed with whatever the cooks in the kitchen decide to put into it that day.

Fatties has transitioned into a stationary restaurant housed in a splendid orange-hued, wood-frame house and outbuilding with an open-air bar and several large picnic tables out back. The Airstream trailer, which has been pretty much retired, sits at a rakish angle next to the picnic area, a reminder of how the whole thing got started. In addition, there are a couple of lovely dining rooms inside the house for the winter months, which can be very busy, given the proximity to the Sugarloaf ski area.

Local brews round out the offerings at this one-of-a-kind spot. The MacMichaels are a delightful couple dedicated to serving locals and tourists alike in a fun, festive, "fatty" kind of way.

268 Main St., Kingfield, 207-399-9246
rollingfatties.com

SHUCK STATION

The top spot for Damariscotta River oysters

One of the first things you see after pulling off Route 1 and driving toward Damariscotta is an old service station converted into a large, open-air oyster bar at the top of Main Street. Though technically in Newcastle, this relatively new eatery has quickly become the focal point for enjoying the bounty of world-class oysters coming from the nearby Damariscotta River.

Shuck Station is the brainchild of Brendan Parsons, a Damariscotta native who became involved in the oyster distribution business. He rented the former Chevron building at the corner of Main and Pump streets, literally a stone's throw from the famed river. As he began handling oysters from nearby oyster farms on the river, he thought it might be fun to put in a small oyster bar at his distributorship and sell some of his wares to the locals. At the same time, he could install several beer taps and sell local suds, further increasing the appeal of his retail experiment. People loved it.

Shuck Station has quickly established itself as the best place to experience all that the Damariscotta River has to offer. The river itself is extremely clean, with no industry or other commercial enterprises compromising the water's quality. In addition, the Great Salt Pond upstream provides the fresh water that helps create the brackishness in the river that's essential for propagating healthy oysters. There are at least a dozen oyster farms between Route 1 and the mouth of the river 11 miles or so to the south, and Shuck Station features bivalves from nearly all of them on an ever-changing basis.

The Shuck Station experience begins with walking across the crushed oyster-shell grounds to the numerous picnic tables and the

Left: Shuck Station's shingle hanging on Main Street.

Top center: Shiitake mushroom bao buns.

Above center: A fence made of Shuck Station oyster shells.

Right: A "Taste of the River."

eight-seat oyster bar. Inside the station's former office and waiting area, there's now a stone counter piled with oysters ready for shucking. The walls are decorated with photos of local oystermen and the names of the farms where they work. Be sure to check out the laminated map of the river showing the names and locations of all the farms.

Ordering is quite simple: you may buy oysters individually, by the half dozen, or dozen. Every day, the Shuck Station puts together a "Taste of the River"—12 oysters, four each from three different farms, specially selected by the staff and served with mignonette and cocktail sauces.

Other comestibles include hot and cold appetizers, a few different salads, and several sandwiches. But face it: oysters are what this plein-air paradise is all about, and it should be what everyone comes to enjoy in this quaint river town.

68 Main St., Newcastle, 207-682-0129

SALVAGE BBQ

Barbecue done right

Salvage BBQ celebrates its 10th anniversary on Portland's west side in 2023, and it has established itself as the preeminent place for barbecue in the city. Housed in the former Portland Architectural Salvage building (hence the name), Salvage BBQ's smokers and industrial-sized kitchen have been delighting diners with all sorts of smoked goodies over the past decade. Traveling west from downtown on Congress Street, keep your eyes peeled for the red and white SALVAGE BBQ sign painted on the side of the brick building. Then follow your nose to the best barbecue in town.

Back in 2012, Jay Villani and Ray Touringhy embarked on a self-guided tour of Texas and North Carolina to experience and research firsthand the magic of barbecue that made both regions famous in their own ways. Taking what they found most appealing from their experiences, the partners returned to Maine and set about locating a spot to launch an authentic Southern barbecue place. The architectural salvage building proved to be the perfect spot, given its cavernous interior and its parking lot in the back where smokers could be set up.

Villani, an experienced welder, purchased an old, massive propane tank and converted it into two industrial-sized smokers that handle most of Salvage's meat cooking. They're located in back of the building under canvas tarps, and smoky barbecue scents waft out into the neighborhood from early morning onward.

The building's interior is a large, open, high-ceilinged room filled with picnic tables for communal dining and supplemented with a handful of smaller formica-top tables. Salvage is a counter-service operation, meaning you queue up at the food counter by the front door, study the chalkboard menu, and order away. If you're

Top left: The motherlode of beer taps.

Above left: The setting at every table.

Top center: Salvage's bold sign on Congress Street is hard to miss.

Above center: The brisket sandwich with barbecue baked beans and pickles.

Right: The restaurant's cavernous interior.

dining in, you'll be given a number on a metal stand, which you post on your table, letting servers know where you are when your food is ready.

The barbecue here is among the finest in New England. The brisket is tender and perfectly smoked and sliced, and may be had straight up or in a sandwich. Another popular meat choice is the St. Louis-style ribs, tender and sweet yet still clinging to the bone. The sides of choice include mac and cheese, homemade slaw, fresh-baked cornbread, and smoky chili.

There are 17 different beers on tap, most of them from local microbreweries. Home-baked pie slices may be had for anyone who still has room for dessert.

919 Congress St., Portland, 207-553-2100
salvagebbq.com

> **To get the full effect of the Salvage experience, order the "Meat Coma," a dizzying platter of ribs, brisket, chopped pork, a bowl of chili, and two sides.**

McLOON'S LOBSTER SHACK

A top-notch lobster shack experience

In the short span of 10+ years, McLoon's Lobster Shack has shot to fame as one of the premier seafood shacks in New England. Thanks to praise from the likes of *Yankee* magazine, other prominent New England media, and word of mouth, McLoon's is blessed with hundreds of customers nearly every day in summertime, despite its somewhat remote location on (car-reachable) Spruce Head Island in South Thomaston. This is a place well worth seeking out for its splendid victuals and gorgeous setting.

McLoon's roots reach back to the 1940s, when McLoon's Wharf came into being as a place where local lobstermen could offload and sell their catch and stock up on bait for their traps. In 2002, the Douty family bought the wharf as an extension of their wholesale seafood business in New Jersey.

Ten years later in 2012, Bree Douty, a young member of the Douty clan, came up with the idea of opening a lobster shack across a small inlet from the wharf and cooking up some of the catch for a dine-in-the-rough seafood eatery. A weathered red shed was converted into a cookhouse, several picnic tables were scattered about the grassy grounds, and McLoon's Lobster Shack was off and running.

Yankee magazine featured a photo of the shack on the cover of their summer 2015 issue, and things haven't been the same since. McLoon's is in a beautiful spot on the edge of a harbor surrounded by islets and forests of pine. In many ways, the view is as good as the food.

The lobster roll at McLoon's takes center stage on the menu. It's why most people make the long trek to see what all the fuss is about, and few, if any, are disappointed. The McLoon's roll consists of four ounces of sweet, tender, fresh-picked tail and claw meat

Top left: McLoon's distinctive shack on Spruce Head Island.
Above left: McLoon's waterside location is sublime.
Right: A lobster roll with all the trimmings.

procured from the adjacent wharf, guaranteeing absolute freshness. The lobster is tucked into a buttered, toasted, top-split hot dog bun with mayo spread on the inside or served with a small cup of melted butter (or both). It's the shack's most popular item.

Other sandwiches include a crabmeat roll, a crab cake sandwich, burgers, and grilled cheese. Also from the grill come roasted littleneck clams with garlic herb butter.

McLoon's season is short—from late May to mid-October—so be sure to make the drive and get in on one of the best spots for lobster in Maine.

315 Island Rd., South Thomaston, 207-593-1382
mcloonslobster.com

PERRY'S LOBSTER SHACK

Home port for a famed female lobster boat captain

This relative newcomer to the lobster shack scene has made a name for itself due to two main factors: its authentic, super-fresh lobster brought in on its own dock daily and its distinction as the home base of Linda Greenlaw, famed local lobster boat captain and author of *The Lobster Chronicles*.

Perry's story is one of those classic shack tales about a family starting a lobster business, and then eventually being persuaded to start cooking up some of their catch right by their dock. Perry, Beverly, and Kathy Long purchased some waterfront property on a spit of land in the town of Surry in 1992. They set up a lobster wholesaling business from their dock and started working with local lobstermen, buying their catch for resale.

As often happens, curious locals and passersby asked if the Longs might consider cooking up some of their catch right by the dock. They gave it a try, setting up a few tables on the shore and using old lobster crates for seating. This funky setup spawned a more refined operation after a couple of years, with picnic tables placed on the long, narrow dock, along with a lovingly carved and shellacked counter and high-top chairs running dockside for folks to belly up and enjoy a lobster dinner while gazing out over the water. (There are distant views of Mount Desert Island to the southeast.)

Linda Greenlaw conducts regular tours on her lobster boat from Perry's dock to take in local scenery from the water and to witness the lobstering life up close.

Left: Wooden dining counters line one side of Perry's dock.

Top center: A lovingly crafted wooden sign graces the side of the shack.

Above center: Perry's lobster dinner.

Right: Perry's charming cook shack.

It didn't take long for word to spread, and Perry's pretty quickly became a destination eatery, made more appealing when Linda Greenlaw declared it home base for her own lobster boat. The family built a modest cook shack, painted it an appealing grey with bright red trim, and expanded the seating on land and the dock to accommodate up to 60 people.

Perry succumbed to cancer after an eight-year battle, and the shack's future became uncertain until grandson, Seth, stepped up to partner with his grandmother, Beverly, to keep the operation alive. Seth has poured heart and soul (and lots of sweat equity) into Perry's to keep it going, and it appears to have paid off well. The shack has garnered national praise, and increasing numbers of lobster lovers are seeking it out during the summer months.

The menu is simple. Lobster and lobster roll dinners are the most popular items. Next come the crabmeat roll and Gram's Lobster Mac 'n' Cheese. Starters include a magnificent crab dip and steamed mussels, and fresh local oysters were recently added. Seth may even install a raw bar in the near future, making Perry's a shack to contend with.

1076 Newbury Neck, Surry, 207-667-1955
perryslobstershack.com

THE LOBSTER SHACK AT TWO LIGHTS

Great seafood, magnificent view

Few seafood shacks (or any restaurants, for that matter) put you as close to Maine's crashing surf as the venerable Lobster Shack at Two Lights, a classic place to enjoy some super fresh seafood and a commanding view of the open ocean.

This seaside shack got its start in the 1920s as a small place called the Lobster Shop, where lobster rolls were the specialty at a time when lobster rolls were just becoming a thing. In 1968, a local baker named Jim Ledbetter and his wife, Ruth, bought the eatery and renamed it the Lobster Shack. The "Two Lights" moniker, referencing a couple of nearby lighthouses, came later and was added to give the shack a more distinctive name.

The Ledbetters expanded the seafood menu, added some grilled items and non-seafood fare, and threw in some baked items, some of which remain on the menu to this day. Some 10 years later, their daughter, Martha, and her husband, Herb Porch, took over the business, and they were succeeded in 2005 by their son, Jeff, and his wife, Katie, who remain owners. It's truly a family operation with many members of the extended family involved in one way or another.

Once you find the place (it isn't easy without GPS), park your car in the lot, and ascend the stone steps, behold the shack's spacious patio with some 30 picnic tables overlooking the sea. The view is mesmerizing but push on to the small building that houses the order counter and a pine-paneled dining room. A staff of workers dressed in kitchen whites stand behind the counter, ready to take your order and cook it up in their compact kitchen.

All victuals are posted on boards by the counter, along with the day's prices for lobster and clam items. Settle up your tab,

Top left: The entryway to the Two Lights seaside patio.

Above left: Two Lights's famed lobster roll, with its signature dollop of mayo.

Top center: The indoor dining room is filled with antiques kitsch.

Above center: Dining by the sea is a windy but wonderful experience.

Right: Fresh-baked goods on display and for sale at the order counter.

get your order number, and then stake out a place to sit on the patio or in the dining room. They'll announce your number over a loudspeaker when your food is ready to pick up.

The lobster roll remains the most popular item at Two Lights. It's a cold roll on a toasted, split-top bun with lobster and a thin piece of lettuce, a pickle slice, and a rather large dollop of mayo that can be mixed in with the lobster or dispensed with, depending on your preference. Melted butter is also available.

The fried seafood is excellent, as are the home-baked desserts. Two Lights is BYO, so feel free to bring beer or wine with you. There's also a nice gift shop worth checking out right next to the patio. It's got some great Maine memorabilia.

225 Two Lights Rd., Cape Elizabeth, 207-799-1677
lobstershacktwolights.com

There's a foghorn stationed right next to the Two Lights patio that issues periodic blasts every 15 seconds when weather conditions warrant.

JESS'S MARKET

The best seafood market in Midcoast Maine

Nothing beats a family-owned seafood market—one that's watched over carefully, that has strong ties to local suppliers, and that gets to know its customers well. Jess's Market is one of those gems, and the tri-town area of Rockland, Rockport, and Camden is very fortunate to have this retailer in their community for all of their seafood needs.

Founded in 1986 by Shannon O'Brien and well into its second generation of family ownership, Jess's is located on a quiet stretch of Rockland's Main Street, away from downtown, as the street begins its journey south toward Owls Head. Owned by O'Brien and managed by her daughters, Lisa Gordon and twins Katie and Jamie Wiggin, this charming, well-organized shop is perfectly set up to handle any seafood needs or desires.

There are two glass cases filled with fresh finned fish and shellfish, most from local fishermen who are direct suppliers to the market. There's cod, haddock, hake, salmon of various types (including smoked), trout, halibut, tuna, swordfish, and more. Seasonal fish like black cod and bluefish are regularly stocked, as are somewhat exotic items like fresh shad and shad roe from the Connecticut River in late spring. Shellfish on display include a variety of clams, mussels, oysters, diver sea scallops, shrimp, and squid.

Nearby are the lobster tanks, bubbling away with hundreds of locally caught lobsters, brought in fresh daily from local lobstermen. Feel free to select your own, or let Jess's knowledgeable

In addition to its popular retail seafood business, Jess's also supplies most of the three-town area's restaurants with their seafood needs.

Top left: Jess's street-side shingle, displaying the specials of the day.

Above left: The lobster tanks are always brimming with red guys.

Top center: There's lots of locally procured seafood in the display cases.

Top right: Jess's carefully selected wines section.

Above right: Jamie Wiggin, Lisa Gordon, and Katie Wiggin—the owner's daughters and the heart and soul of the market.

staff pick for you. They will cook your "bugs" on the premises for a few bucks more, or you may take them home to cook on your own.

Next to the lobster tanks is a nook filled with carefully curated wines, one of the best selections in Rockport. Local craft brews as well as a variety of gourmet cheeses and other goodies may be found in refrigerated cases against a couple of the walls. And several wire shelving units in the middle of the store offer all sorts of gourmet crackers, coffees, teas, cookies, and more.

Have questions or need suggestions? The attentive staff behind the counter can handle just about any need you may have. Be sure to check this place out when in the Rockland area, as it's the best place in the area to get fresh seafood.

118 South Main St., Rockland, 207-596-6068
jessmarket.com

THURSTON'S LOBSTER POUND

Two levels of lobster fun overlooking Bass Harbor

Jutting out over Bass Harbor in a two-level, screened-in, yellow-roofed building on a sturdy dock, Thurston's Lobster Pound is certainly one of the most scenic and authentic places in the state to enjoy whole lobster, lobster rolls, and more. This out-of-the-way eatery in tiny Bernard, Maine, is definitely worth the trip all the way out to the southwestern corner of Mount Desert Island.

The restaurant is an offshoot of the adjacent wholesale lobster business, a family operation that goes back five generations. Fred Thurston founded the F. W. Thurston Company in 1946, and since then, various branches of the Thurston family have sold fuel, bait, and supplies to a sizeable fleet of lobster boats from their pier.

The restaurant came into being in 1993 when fourth-generation family member Michael Radcliffe and his wife, Elizabeth, created Thurston's Lobster Pound on an adjacent pier. Initially just a one-level operation hovering on piles high above the harbor waters, the couple built out a second, lower level to accommodate the crowds showing up every summer.

It's quite a sight to drive up and behold the yellow-roofed, two-tier restaurant hovering over the harbor. If you happen to arrive at lunchtime, there's a changing of the guard, as lobstermen depart in their trucks after a long morning of fishing, and restaurant patrons grab parking places as they become available. Be sure to take note of the large, lidded boiling pot positioned on the restaurant's front porch as you enter.

Top left: Thurston's distinctive, two-tiered shack hanging over Bass Harbor.
Above left: Thurston's snagged this coveted vanity plate years ago.
Top right: Thurston's lobster dinner with all the trimmings.
Above right: The dining areas are bathed in a golden hue from the awnings.

Whole lobster is the recommended way to go at Thurston's, given the beautiful outdoor setting next to the lobster dock. The lobsters come in three different sizes, and you may choose between hard-shell (fully formed) and soft-shell (recently molted, new-shell) lobsters. There's more meat per pound in the hard shells, but the meat in the soft shells tends to be sweeter and more tender. Lobster dinners may be accompanied by a pound of steamed clams or mussels, corn on the cob, coleslaw, and a thick bread-like square of blueberry cake.

Thurston's is BYO, so be sure to bring along your cooler of libations and get ready to spend a glorious hour or two suspended above the harbor in this little slice of lobster heaven.

9 Thurston Rd., Bernard, 207-244-7600
thurstonforlobster.com

LAKESHORE HOUSE

A port in the storm for AT hikers, locals, and lucky passersby

The town of Monson is at a key juncture of the Appalachian Trail. It's a few miles from the southern terminus of the 100-Mile Wilderness, a stretch of the trail where there's essentially nothing in the way of civilization or amenities to the northeast. Hikers, whether traveling north or south, need to bring along at least a week's worth of provisions in order to make it through. Monson is there to comfort hikers before or after they hike the 100-mile gauntlet.

Lakeshore House Pub and Lodge is located on Main Street across from the regional Appalachian Trail information center. The house is a beacon of hope and help, and it has a wonderful restaurant that serves up good food and drink to hikers and anyone else. It's in a white, well-aged frame house that backs up on scenic Lake Hebron. Lakeshore is a year-round operation, serving hikers and anglers in the warmer months and hunters and snowmobilers in the chilly seasons.

Rebekah Anderson first opened Lakeshore House in the summer of 2006, with a modest pub, a few hostel-like rooms on the second floor, and a laundromat next to the pub on the first floor. The enterprise was popular from the get-go, and Rebekah kept making improvements over the years, including an upgrade and expansion of the kitchen and a conversion of the laundromat into a dining room. Nick Fusco and Erin Miller purchased the lodge and pub in 2021, keeping the good vibes going.

Perhaps the best time to grab a meal at Lakeshore is in the summer, when the establishment's backyard serves as a colorful dining area overlooking the lake. It's a very laid-back atmosphere, with lots of congeniality between dining parties and the youthful

Left: The quaint pub.

Top center: Brightly colored tables in back by the lake.

Above center: The New Wave Salad.

Top right: Lakeshore House—restaurant below, lodging above.

Above right: The Jolly Roger flies over Lakeshore House's dock.

waitstaff. All the tables and chairs are painted in bright colors, and most of the tables have umbrellas, providing respite from the midsummer sun. The quaint, wood-countered pub inside is open year-round and has open-mic night every Thursday.

Now for the food. Things tend to be on the healthy side, with several salads that serve well as full meals. The New Wave Salad features chicken marinated in teriyaki and served over a bed of lettuce, sugared walnuts, Craisins, and shaved Asiago cheese. The bruschetta is a great opener, made with sourdough bread slathered with pesto, chunks of fresh mozzarella and tomatoes, olive oil, and salt and pepper. The pub is a full-service bar with several local brews on tap.

9 Tenney Hill Rd., Monson, 207-997-7069
thelakeshorehouse.com

CONGDON'S DOUGHNUTS

Congdon's is the (not so little) doughnut shop that could.

In its many lives and permutations, Congdon's famed doughnuts and other breakfast fare have held a firm grip on the appetites and imaginations of locals and tourists alike in Southern Maine. With a history stretching back more than 75 years, Congdon's continues to reinvent itself, much to the delight of its customers.

Back in 1945, Clint and Dot ("Nana") Congdon opened Congdon's Restaurant on Main Street in Kennebunk, where the place established a reputation for fine homemade doughnuts. Ten years later, Nana and her son-in-law, Herb Brooks, opened Congdon's Doughnuts on the Post Road spot in Wells where it is today. A sit-down restaurant was added (and eventually closed), and satellite doughnut operations were launched in a few nearby towns. Herb died in a plane crash in 1965, and his sister Eleanor took over the business. A fire in 1979 destroyed the Wells doughnut stand, which was then rebuilt, along with a small indoor dining area for year-round service. Another fire in 1983 temporarily closed Congdon's in the midst of its busy summer season.

More recently, the pandemic forced Congdon's to be a drive-through, takeaway stand only until it completely reopened in the spring of 2022. Throughout its travails, the extended Congdon, Brooks, and Leech families have been able to keep serving its amazing doughnuts indoors and out.

After entering through Congdon's front door, queue up before shelves packed with wire racks filled with fresh-cooked doughnuts. Most regulars order by the half dozen or baker's dozen, both of which come in colorful Congdon's cardboard boxes.

Choosing what to order is a challenge, as there are so many wonderful treats on display. There are two basic types of doughnuts,

Top left: Congdon's big sign out front on Route 1.

Above left: A half-dozen, boxed and ready to go.

Top right: There are plenty of tempting treats on Congdon's doughnut racks.

Above right: A photo on the wall of Congdon's, showing an earlier version of the eatery.

each type coming in a variety of flavors and textures. The plain doughnuts are simple and straightforward, made with wet batter, and come in nine varieties. Then there are the raised doughnuts, which are hand-cut, fluffier, and often glazed with a sweet, sugary coating. Many of the 20 raised doughnut types contain fillings of jelly, cream, peanut butter, and more. Toppings include such tempting fare as sprinkles and shredded coconut.

Summer is the busiest season, and it's great to grab a picnic table out front along Route 1 and watch the traffic flow by. The newly reopened indoor dining room brings comfort on cold and rainy days. But a box of Congdon's finest may even be enjoyed while sitting in your car in the parking lot or back home, wherever that may be.

1090 Post Road, Wells, 207-646-4219
congdons.com

During the summer months, Congdon's has a food truck park in the lot next to their restaurant. More than a dozen food trucks serve up food and snacks of all types, along with a beer garden and live entertainment.

BROWNE TRADING COMPANY

A top place for high-end seafood

World-renowned caviar. Top-notch fresh and smoked seafood. An amazing collection of wines. These are the hallmarks of Browne Trading Company, one of the leading gourmet seafood retailers in the country.

The Browne story goes back to the early 1800s, when John Brown (the "e" was added around the time of the Civil War) set up a fishing operation on the Kennebec River north of Brunswick. Brown and his descendants became particularly known for harvesting caviar from the sturgeon in the river.

Fast forward to 1979, when Rod Browne Mitchell, a recent college grad, passionate gourmet, and avid fisherman, opened a wine and cheese shop in Camden. He eventually started carrying caviar from around the world in his shop, selling retail to customers and wholesale to some of the best chefs and restaurants in the country. It wasn't long before he was the go-to source for caviar, Maine diver scallops, and peekytoe crabmeat for famed chefs like Eric Ripert, Daniel Boulud, and Thomas Keller.

In 1991, Rod and his wife decided to move their operation to a lovely brick building on the Portland waterfront, right next to famed Merrill's Wharf. In addition to the caviar and gourmet seafood, Browne's began smoking much of its fish in state-of-the-art ovens in a large building adjacent to the storefront. They also opened a retail fish market, adding gourmet foods and cheeses and a vast wine selection to the mix.

When you enter the market, there are two large glass cases—the one on the left, featuring caviars, oysters, and various shellfish,

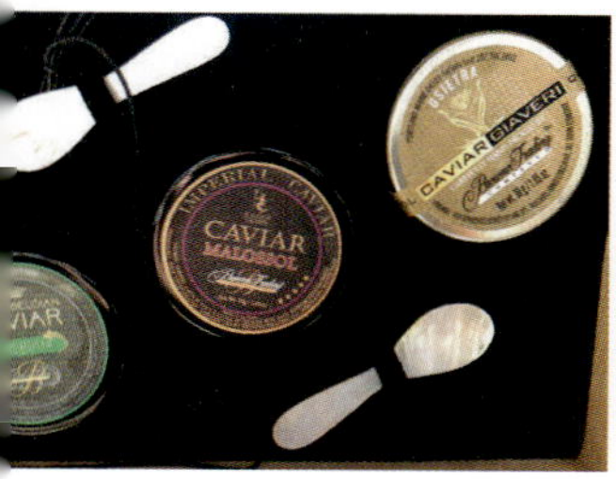

Top left: Browne's handsome brick building on Commercial Street in Portland.
Above left: A small sampling of Browne's renowned caviar holdings.
Top center: There are lots of whole and filleted fish in Browne's cases every day.
Above center: Browne Trading Company is the choice supplier for many of the nation's top chefs.
Right: Fresh and shucked oysters on ice.

and the one on the right, showcasing beautiful whole fish (mostly salmon from around the world) and loads of fish fillets mostly of local origin.

The other half of the ground floor contains refrigerated cases filled with cheeses and wire shelves loaded with all sorts of gourmet goodies, from crackers to sea salts to pickles and more. Go up one level and behold a sea of wooden racks displaying thousands of bottles of wine of every origin and vintage imaginable, all curated by Browne's knowledgeable staff.

Most of the caviar is stored in refrigerated vaults in the back building, but serious buyers are encouraged to inquire what's currently available and to purchase from a wide selection of the world's finest. And the smoked fish is second to none. It comes in the form of salmon, trout, shrimp, mussels, and sea scallops.

Come to Browne Trading for the best of everything in seafood and more.

262 Commercial St., Portland, 207-775-7560
brownetrading.com

VASQUEZ MEXICAN TAKEOUT

Real-deal Mexican fare in a Downeast setting

Should you tire of the splendid seafood that Maine's Downeast coast offers up every summer, consider a stop at Vasquez Mexican Takeout on Route 1 in Milbridge, an ethnic oasis in the heart of Maine's seafood kingdom.

This bright green roadside food emporium began life as a bus parked at the Wyman & Son blueberry fields in nearby Deblois. Over the years, hundreds of migrant Mexican workers have picked blueberries in the fields during late summer and early fall. The Vasquez family was initially part of the seasonal picking crews, and then a couple of the Vasquez women started cooking up Mexican fare to feed their family and other workers. They rigged up an old bus with cooking appliances in the early 2000s and started a mobile kitchen long before the food truck craze.

Fast forward to today, and the Vasquez clan has an established takeout eatery attached to a white house on Route 1 in downtown Milbridge. The two-story structure is painted a bright green with an enclosed eating area and a dozen or so picnic tables scattered about the grounds. The still-seasonal enterprise has been warmly received by locals and tourists alike, serving up authentic Mexican fare in large quantities at very affordable prices.

Step inside to place your order through a colorful window that also offers a glimpse into the busy kitchen where the cooks work their magic on the stovetops and ovens within. The bulk of the menu

The *Portland Press Herald* once claimed that the Vazquez Mexican Takeout burritos are every bit as good as the ones available in Portland–and at half the price.

Left: The indoor dining area.

Center: The Mexican Plate, with a little bit of everything.

Right: Vasquez's distinctive green building on Route 1.

is familiar Mexican fare, such as tacos, burritos, quesadillas, and chimichangas, all served in gargantuan quantities. The same goes for the side orders of refried beans and yellow rice, both of which may be considered meals in themselves. Thankfully, nearly everything is served up in sturdy, lidded containers, so what you cannot finish may be easily transported home.

It's unusual to find such a large Latino food operation so far from its food distribution sources, but the Vasquez family has worked hard to find the right suppliers in order to make their fare as authentic as possible. Their flour and corn tortillas are homemade, as are their spicy, flavorful red and green salsas, which come with every dish. Most dishes include a choice of well-prepared meats such as beef, steak, pork, chicken, or chorizo, adding yet more to the authenticity of the place.

Though Vasquez remains essentially a seasonal restaurant, it hopes someday to be more year-round while continuing to serve the seasonal migrant population that helped spawn their successful business in the first place.

38 Main St., Milbridge, 207-546-2219

THE RED BARN

Good music, great food, and well-deserved praise for military vets

Few restaurants in Maine are as red, white, and blue (or as giving) as the Red Barn of Augusta. Owned and led by the indefatigable Laura Benedict, the nearly 50-year-old eatery on Riverside Drive serves as an inspiration, a gathering place, and a nifty spot for Augustans and many others to gather, eat good food, and participate in dozens of different charitable causes sponsored by the restaurant.

The Red Barn was founded in 1977 by Bill and Florence Benedict with the idea of serving great fried chicken nuggets and seafood to locals and passersby on the busy highway. After some initial success, the incursion of chain restaurants around Augusta took a big bite out of the Red Barn's business. Enter Laura Benedict, Bill's younger sister, who bought the struggling restaurant from her brother and took on the challenge of turning it around. At the same time, Laura was struggling with an alcohol problem, which she overcame, and she emerged as a person transformed. Dedicating herself to the restaurant's success, her sobriety, and to giving back to the community she loves so much, Laura has built a juggernaut of a restaurant and a huge fundraising organization to boot, raising more than $2 million to date for a wide variety of causes.

Veterans and their welfare are a leading cause to which the Red Barn has committed itself. It shows in all the tributes posted on the walls and in the signage posted throughout the Red Barn's multi-acre property. Those in uniform, active and retired, are treated like royalty here, and this has resonated positively throughout the state.

With regard to the restaurant and its victuals, the Red Barn is a clean, efficiently run fried food shack with large grounds for dining and for hosting frequent live entertainment that appears on

Top left: One of many displays honoring military veterans.

Above left: The Red Barn, an Augusta institution.

Above center: The Red Barn's Mixed Seafood Basket.

Top right: One of the spacious outdoor dining areas.

Above right: The Red Barn prides itself on its chicken offerings as well as seafood.

a couple of small stages on the property. The place has the look and feel of a small county fair.

As for the food, it's cooked to order, efficiently served, and surprisingly tasty for a place that's dozens of miles from the coast. Nearly everything is breaded with a light crumb coating and deep fried to perfection. Portions are generous, and the prices more than fair. Check this place out for its fine victuals and for its unerring efforts to give thanks and to help others in need.

455 Riverside Dr., Augusta, 207-623-9485
theredbarnmaine.org

CHAUNCEY CREEK LOBSTER PIER

Lots of creek-side color (and loads of lobster)

Should you wish to get far from the madding crowds populating Kittery's outlet strip in the summer, head to nearby Kittery Point and seek out Chauncey Creek Lobster Pier, one of the premier lobster shacks in Southern Maine.

The pier was originally constructed on the tidal creek in the 1930s by lobsterman Herb Whitman and served as a place for lobster boats to stack traps, offload their lobster catches, and refuel. Curious locals started asking if Whitman could cook up some of the lobster, and Whitman's son-in-law, George Spinney, obliged by installing boilers and lobster tanks. An increasing number of picnic tables started popping up on the pier, and eventually the transition from dock to lobster shack was complete. Today, George's son, Ron, owns Chauncey Creek Lobster, taking over in 1984 and running it with the help of his family ever since.

The shack is located on a side road off Route 103 and is tucked into the creek bank, partially obscured by bushes and trees. Park your car along the roadside and descend a staircase to the pier where numerous brightly painted picnic tables and a couple of red shacks beckon. The sparkling creek makes for a lovely backdrop, and boaters tie up for lunch and dinner throughout the day.

The atmosphere on the pier is one of informal conviviality. Chauncey Creek is a "dine in the rough" operation, meaning you order your food through an open window at one of the sheds, then grab a table and wait for your order to be ready. The shack is BYO for alcohol as well as side dishes and desserts, as long as it's not something that's also on the shack's menu. People bring leafy

Top left: Chauncey Creek's lobster roll, served on an unorthodox round bun.
Above left: The pier is always lively in the summertime.
Center: A crate of lobsters being lowered onto the pier.
Top right: The roadside sign that lets you know you've arrived at Chauncey Creek.
Above right: Lobsters are served up by the trayful for large parties.

salads, desserts, and oftentimes tablecloths and elaborate tableware to fancy up their meals.

What's cooking in the sheds? Whole boiled lobster is the most popular item. Feel free to go into the lobster shed and pick your own or specify what size you'd like. The lobster roll, based on the recipe developed by Ron's mother, is also very popular. Chowder, chili, and steamed mussels and clams are popular starters, as are fresh-shucked clams, oysters, and boiled shrimp.

Chauncey Creek is very tidal, rising and falling several feet each day, and it makes for a great place to watch boaters of all sorts glide by. The shack presents a completely different side of Kittery, one that those in the know find peaceful and relaxing.

16 Chauncey Creek Road, Kittery, 207-439-1030
chaunceycreek.com

THE HOLY DONUT

Made from homegrown Aroostook County spuds

Maine is known for its potatoes, and now, thanks to the Holy Donut, it's also getting attention for its delectable Maine potato donuts. Lots of eyebrows were raised in 2010 when Leigh Kellis, a resident of Portland's Munjoy Hill neighborhood, began experimenting with doughnut recipes in her kitchen. She was captivated by the use of riced potatoes as the basis for the doughnuts. She goosed the recipe around until she hit on her preferred flavor and texture. The Holy Donut was born, and some dozen years, three locations, and 150 employees later, Kellis's dream has been more than fulfilled.

What exactly is a Holy Donut? Leigh's recipe calls for unbleached flour, local buttermilk, New England eggs, and Aroostook County potatoes. The potatoes are boiled, pressed through a ricer, and then incorporated into the mix. The dough is rolled out, sliced into rounds, and each doughnut is fried until golden brown.

Coffee by Design, a local Portland coffee shop, was the first outlet to give Leigh's doughnuts a chance, allowing her to bring in a couple dozen each day to sell to customers. Word spread about this unique new, homegrown taste treat, and other retailers lined up to get in on the action. Leigh rented some commercial kitchen space and ramped up her production with the initial help of her father.

Eventually the opportunity to open a freestanding Holy Donut shop became a reality in 2012 when Leigh's mother bravely offered her retirement savings to bankroll their first store at 194 Park Avenue, not far from Hadlock Field, home of the Portland Sea Dogs minor league baseball team. A second retail spot, on Exchange Street in the Old Port, opened shortly thereafter. In the meantime, dougnut recipes and variations were rolled out from

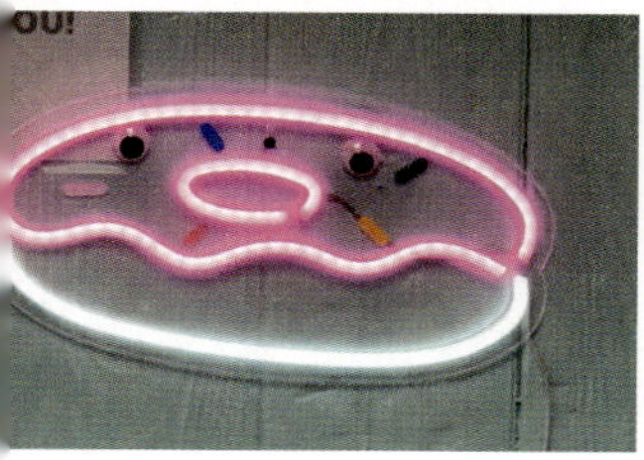

Top left: Some of the many doughnut flavors offered each day.

Above left: A neon doughnut graces the wall at the Park Avenue shop.

Top center: Holy Donut's original store on Portland's Park Avenue.

Above center: Holy Donut has its own brand of dark roast coffee from Wicked Joe coffees.

Right: The Maple and Chocolate Sea Salt doughnuts.

the kitchen, to the point where there are some two dozen different doughnut varieties today.

Walking into a Holy Donut store is as much a feast for the eyes as it is for the palette. Racks of colorfully iced doughnuts sit just behind the order counter, beckoning customers to ogle the offerings and start ordering away. Perhaps the best-known Holy Donut is the Dark Chocolate Sea Salt, a sinfully rich, tasty, and addictive morsel that's as good for your dinner dessert as it is for a breakfast treat. Two other top sellers are the maple doughnuts and the scarlet-colored triple berry dougnut.

Coffee is fresh-brewed here throughout the day, using fair-trade beans custom roasted for Holy Donut. Though the Exchange Street outlet recently closed, a new store opened on Commercial Street. And since 2017, nearby Scarborough has been blessed with a Holy Donut megastore of sorts, right on busy Route 1.

194 Park Ave., Portland, 207-874-7774
177 Commercial St., Portland, 207-331-5655
398 Route 1, Scarborough, 207-303-0137
theholydonut.com

CAMERON'S LOBSTER HOUSE

The world's only drive-in lobster shack

Classic drive-in restaurants with car-hop service are a rarity these days, but even rarer is a drive-in lobster shack. Cameron's Lobster House is a clever take on the drive-in tradition: just pull into one of the covered parking spaces, turn on your headlights, and a server will be out momentarily to take your order.

The drive-in has been owned by Dana Cameron since 2006, and prior to that time, a restaurant named Morse's occupied the space. Cameron has kept many of the more charming elements of the drive-in architecture (a lengthy carport providing shelter for car-hop diners, retro signage advertising specials and side dishes, and large, slanted picture windows in the dining room), while updating the eating areas with solid wood furniture inside and a breezy covered deck with wrought-iron tables and chairs along the building's side.

The most popular lobster dish here is, of course, the lobster roll. It comes in two sizes (go with the larger version), and it may be had either chilled with mayo or warmed with butter. Both versions are served on a toasted, buttered bun and come with chips and a pickle. For a few dollars more, two sides may be substituted. Go with the crispy onion rings and the cup of home-baked beans featuring kidney and navy beans in a heady sauce.

Lobster may also be found in the lobster stew, and whole steamed lobster dinners are available at dinnertime and come with corn, coleslaw, fries, and a dinner roll. (Best to enjoy this indoors or on the deck and not while sitting in your car.) And Cameron's is particularly proud of its hefty lobster BLT sandwich.

Left: A lobster roll with a couple of sides.

Top right: Cameron's lobster house drive-in.

Center right: The much-coveted circular dining booth.

Above right: Turn your headlights on for car-side service.

Salads come with or without various seafood adornments, such as fried shrimp, crab meat, lobster, scallops, and even fried haddock. For those looking to sidestep seafood, there are burgers, wraps, hot dogs, and chicken fingers.

The service is very friendly and attentive, befitting a well-run family operation. Should you have a party of four to six, try to snag the circular booth in the dining room, the only throwback seating indoors from the restaurant's earlier days.

Haute cuisine this is not, but Cameron's provides good meals at fair prices, and it offers car-hop service for those wishing to take a step back in time.

18 Bath Rd., Brunswick, 207-725-2886
cameronslobsterhouse.com

THE CAPTAIN'S CATCH

That little white shack on the water

Castine is a seafaring town if ever there was one. Located at the end of a peninsula extending southward into the eastern portion of Penobscot Bay, the town's quaint main street and surrounding lanes are lined with the homes of sea captains from days gone by. Castine is also home to the Maine Maritime Academy, a highly regarded state college that provides training for future ocean-bound and land-based maritime workers.

The perfect place to go for a midday meal in Castine is the Captain's Catch, a modest, whitewashed shack located on the town's municipal pier at the base of Main Street. It's a standard dine-in-the-rough operation, where you order your food at one window and pick it up through another when your order number is called. As the name implies, seafood is the specialty here, and Captain's Catch delivers great meals and snacks that are perfect for waterside dining.

The seafood shack opened its doors in 2018, taking over the spot previously occupied by the Dudley's Refresher food stand. Co-owners Walt Foster and Deb Hamblen wanted to offer fresh seafood and other distinctive Maine eats, such as Gifford's ice cream and the bright, red hot dogs known as "snappers."

The menu today still offers the ice cream and red dogs along with a wide variety of seafood treats (especially crab), grilled sandwiches, and seafood salads. Crabmeat pies are the signature dish—individual-sized pastries loaded with fresh-picked crab meat and served with coleslaw. Lobster rolls are the shack's next most popular item, offering a generous portion of chilled lobster meat mixed with a bit of mayo. The crabmeat roll is also popular.

Left: The *Lil' Toot*, a harbor tour boat, docks by Captain's Catch.

Top center: Lobster rolls and fish tacos.

Above center: The town dock also serves as the shack's dining area.

Top right: The Captain's Catch, right next to Castine's town dock.

Above right: The highly popular Crabmeat Pie.

Then there's the unusual and alluring CLOBster roll, an inventive combination of lobster and crab meat packed into a split-top hot dog bun. Grilled sandwiches to consider include the lobster grilled cheese, hamburgers, cheeseburgers, and hot dogs of the red snapper and plain varieties.

There are plenty of tables and other seating right on the town pier, with splendid views of the harbor and all the watercraft anchored there. The *State of Maine*, a large training vessel for the academy students, is docked adjacent to the pier and shack and is a sight to behold on a sunny summer day. This is the best place to enjoy Castine's wonderful waterfront.

5 Sea St., Castine, 207-460-4212

VILLAGE INN AND TAVERN

It's all about the duck.

There's a lot of history at the Village Inn and Tavern—and a lot of good food and drink as well. This year-round gathering place in the village of Belgrade Lakes has been around for over 100 years, offering food and lodging to hunters and fishermen in the days of yore, and now to all types of travelers. And the Village Tavern's most renowned dish is its famed 12-hour roast duck.

The inn initially opened as the Locust's House in 1921, serving seasonal sportsmen fishing the famed Belgrade Lakes and tracking game in the surrounding forests. Nearby Great Pond served as a vacation destination for such famed folks as playwright Eugene O'Neill and the Bean brothers of L. L. Bean fame. The pond also served as inspiration for playwright Ernest Thompson's award-winning play and subsequent film, *On Golden Pond*.

The inn and tavern today is a handsome, two-story, white clapboard building on Main Street. Enter through the front door and find yourself in the warm comfort of a great room, a dining room with windows overlooking a watery scene in back, and nicely appointed antiques throughout. A staircase descends to another dining area with a more pub-like look and feel. Continue through wide back doors below to an outdoor dining area, where numerous picnic tables overlook a channel connecting Great and Long Ponds. Several short docks in the channel allow tavern patrons to arrive by boat.

Want to spend the night? The inn offers six cottage rooms and two two-bedroom "camp quarters," along with a swimming dock for overnight guests.

Left: The warm, charming upper dining room.
Center: The quarter duck with sides and dipping sauces.
Right: The Village's sign out front on Main Street.

Dining here is a real treat, especially in summer when the backyard area is buzzing with activity. Chef Colby Weeks has put together an innovative selection of appetizers and main courses that defy easy culinary categorization or style. One fun starter is the charred shishito peppers, grown in the Village's garden and garnished with togarashi spices. Prosciutto-wrapped medjool dates are another exotic option.

Then there's the duck. It's prepared Peking style and oven roasted for 12 hours. There are five sauces available: blueberry, ginger, black cherry, orange, and peppercorn—order just one for a topping or more than one for dipping on the side. The skin is crispy and flavorful, and the meat tender and juicy. Garlic mashed potatoes and buttered string beans come as sides, and a crispy brown bread stuffing may be added. It's quite a feast. (A quarter-duck portion suffices for most people.)

There's live music a couple of nights a week on the back lawn in the summer, an additional draw for those wishing to dine al fresco.

157 Main St., Belgrade Lakes, 207-495-3553
villageinnandtavern.com

MAINE DINER

A must-stop for those arriving or departing the Pine Tree State

The Maine Diner's first customer was an inebriated driver who crashed into a pole outside the restaurant during a snowstorm in the winter of 1983. The tippler stopped in to sober up with some breakfast and hot coffee. Forty more customers were served that day, and then 100 more the next. Since then, the Maine Diner has served over 8 million customers, many of them regulars, be they locals or frequent visitors to Maine.

Brothers Myles and Dick Henry bought the Maine Diner and its half-acre garden plot in 1983 from Socrates "Louie" Toton, who used to own another diner in Boston. The Henrys started with Louie's menu, supplemented by some recipes from the Henrys' mother and grandmother, and the offerings have grown steadily since.

Louie ran his diner as a sort of personal retirement village, where he could serve customers and garden at the same time. In totally counterintuitive fashion, Louie's diner was open from September through May, shutting down in summertime so he could do his gardening. Summer is the lifeblood of every Maine restaurant, and the Henry brothers went year-round right away.

There are a few dishes that the Henrys introduced to the menu that have brought them national fame, most notably their seafood chowder, lobster pie, and cod cakes. Myles came up with the recipe for the chowder, which is loaded with lots of fresh seafood (lobster, clams, and shrimp), diced potatoes, salt pork, onions, and lots of seasonings. It also calls for equal parts light cream and milk, making it a less thick and more flavorful broth.

The lobster pie recipe originated from the Henrys' grandmother and is perhaps the diner's most popular dish. It consists of fresh-

Top left: The Maine Diner's colorful exterior.

Above left: Homemade Indian pudding.

Top center: The Maine Diner's famed lobster pie.

Above center: The diner's busy counter and dining room.

Right: A colorful neon clock hangs on the wall in the main dining room.

picked lobster meat, crushed Ritz crackers, butter, and lemon, mixed together, then cooked in individual baking dishes.

The diner itself doesn't bear the look of many classic chrome-and-glass eateries of yore. It's housed in a single-story, white building with blue awnings. There is, however, a warm and friendly feeling inside, augmented by the helpful waitstaff, many of whom have worked there for decades. The garden is still out back, supplying the diner with fresh veg during the growing season.

Myles Henry passed away in 2010, and Dick sold the diner to longtime general manager Jim MacNeill in 2018 before retiring, guaranteeing many more years of the Maine Diner's fine food and service.

2265 Post Road, Wells, 207-646-4441
mainediner.com

The Maine Diner has a wonderful gift shop, Remember the Maine, in a building next to the diner. It's a great place to shop for all things Maine.

NUNAN'S LOBSTER HUT

"We Catch 'Em, We Cook 'Em, We Crack 'Em, You Eat 'Em"

Change is inevitable in the restaurant business. However, some of the best restaurants are those that don't change at all, sticking to their tried-and-true methods and warm hospitality, bringing success year after year. Nunan's Lobster Hut is one of those special places.

Located a couple of miles northeast of downtown Kennebunkport in the tiny hamlet of Cape Porpoise, Nunan's is immediately recognizable, with its weathered, shack-like appearance and its brightly painted yellow doors and red window frames. It looks every bit the way one would expect an authentic Maine lobster shack to look. And Nunan's is certainly that.

Nunan's story began in the early 1950s, when family patriarch George Nunan returned from years of fishing Canada's Grand Banks to his home in Cape Porpoise, where he took up lobster and mackerel fishing. In 1951, he started cooking up some of his lobster catch in front of his home, and soon he couldn't keep up with demand from local customers. He converted his workshop into a kitchen in 1953 and an adjacent garage into a dining area. Thus Nunan's was born. The kitchen is still housed in the old workshop, and the dining room has been expanded a couple of times toward the marshland in back.

George's son, Clayton, was also a lobsterman, and he and his wife, Bertha, began helping out in the kitchen in the mid-1950s. Bertha started baking pies to serve for dessert, a tradition she continued for many years. Bertha's sons, Richard (aka "Yogi") and Keith, and their wives have joined and taken over the business for the past three decades. The sons still go lobstering every day and

Left: Homemade strawberry shortcake.

Top center: Nunan's brightly colored exterior is hard to miss from the road.

Above center: A plate of twin boiled lobsters.

Right: Yogi Nunan.

help out in the kitchen at night. Keith's wife, Kim, has carried on the pie-baking tradition.

Lobster is, of course, the focus of the menu at Nunan's. Whole lobsters are boiled in the kitchen and served on rimmed tin plates with lots of butter, potato chips, a dinner roll, and pickles. Lobster stew is thick and creamy and made fresh daily. The lobster roll is meaty and served on a toasted, buttered bun.

One of the best things about Nunan's is dining in its long, narrow dining room, which stretches back shotgun-style from the front door. The ceilings are low, the windows are raised, and cool breezes come in off the marsh.

9 Mills Rd., Kennebunkport, 207-967-4362
nunanslobsterhut.com

It's estimated that Bertha Nunan baked over 80,000 pies during her years in Nunan's kitchen. Her blueberry was the most popular, and her recipe is still used today.

RED'S EATS

A world-famous lobster roll at a classic Maine roadside stand

This diminutive shack on Route 1 next to the Sheepscot River in Wiscasset is so popular that it causes traffic jams nearly every day in the summer, with its long line of customers waiting to order and carloads of passersby gawking at the landmark eatery. Why all the fuss? Red's lobster roll.

The Red's Eats food stand started life in the late 1930s in nearby Boothbay Harbor. It resided there for 16 years before being bought by Allen Gagnon, who moved the eatery to its current spot at the foot of the bridge traversing the Sheepscot River. Al was nicknamed "Red," because he bought Red's Eats, and not the other way around. Gagnon developed the limited menu that's available today, and his amply laden lobster roll, heaped with fresh-picked lobster meat, a piece of lettuce, a toasted, buttered New England-style hot dog bun, and mayo and melted butter on the side became an immediate hit.

The Red's experience starts at the back of a line that winds its way down the sidewalk around Route 1 and oftentimes wraps its way in back of the shack, along freight tracks that still see the occasional train chug by at night. Be prepared to wait at least an hour on pretty much any day in the summertime. It's a good time to strike up conversations, make new friends, or just surf the web

There's a fun little book, co-authored by Red's daughter and current owner, Debbie Cronk, that's titled *Red's Eats: World's Best Lobster Shack*. It's for sale at Red's and at bookstores throughout Maine.

Top left: Red's Eats on a typical summer day.
Above left: A basket of Red's crispy fried clams.
Top right: Red's renowned lobster roll.
Above right: Red's lengthy, slow-moving line.

on your cell phone. Once you make it to the window, place your order, pay your bill, and walk around back where there are some tables and other places to sit. Your number will be called over the intercom, and then you fetch your goodies on a plastic tray and dig into your feast out back.

Any grumbling from customers about the long wait evaporates once the tin foil-wrapped lobster rolls are unsheathed and tucked into. There's a ton of lobster meat—enough that most customers dip pieces into the mayo and butter cups before dressing the entire sandwich. It's quite a feast and doesn't need to be supplemented by much, though a cup of the homemade chowder pairs very nicely with the roll.

Other taste treats at Red's include their famous fried clams, locally sourced, crispy, and sweet. There are several types of seafood baskets and some excellent hot dogs and burgers done in a variety of styles. But it would be a crime to come to Red's and not have their world-famous lobster roll.

41 Main St., Wiscasset, 207-882-6128
redseatsmaine.com

MOODY'S DINER

A Midcoast Maine classic

If you were to play Word Association with just about anybody in Maine and say "Moody's Diner," 99 out of 100 respondents would most likely respond, "Pie!" This venerable eatery, located on a rise along Route 1 in Waldoboro between Damariscotta and Rockland, has been serving up amazing pie and comfort food for nearly a hundred years, and it's currently in its third and fourth generations of Moody family ownership. It's a must-stop for anyone traveling through Midcoast Maine and a genuine slice of Americana a la mode.

Moody's actually started as a few rental cabins built by founder Percy Moody along the old Route 1 in Waldoboro in the 1920s. A dining room and roadside lunch wagon were added to more fully serve the increasing number of car travelers on the highway when it was relocated to its current location. The lunch wagon became a roadside diner and has grown many times over the years into the 100 plus–seat diner it is today.

Moody's is housed in a cavernous, roadhouse-style building that has been remodeled and expanded numerous times over the years. Upon entering, there's a lengthy counter and several booths to the left and a sea of tables and booths to the right. Be sure to check out the photos on the walls to see the history of the diner and the Moody family.

Several of the diner's current dishes may be traced back to matriarch founder Bertha Moody, including the doughnut and pie crust recipes, which still call for lard, the source of much of the great flavor in Moody's baking. Pie types and flavors are numerous and include blueberry, apple, four-berry, walnut, banana cream, chocolate cream, and lemon meringue. Homemade whoopie pies are another specialty.

Left: Current Moody's Diner owner Dan Beck and his manager niece, Linsey Moody.

Top center: Moody's Diner, with its famed neon sign.

Above center: New England Boiled Dinner, a longtime Thursday night special.

Right: A slice of Moody's famed blueberry pie.

Breakfast fare runs the gamut from eggs and toast with bacon or sausage to pancakes, French toast, omelets, and biscuits with sausage gravy. Doughnuts are homemade, fried up daily, and come in plain, cinnamon, and chocolate. The midday menu features a variety of sandwiches and burgers, including the famous Percy Burger, a half-pound of beef topped with grilled mushrooms and Swiss cheese.

Daily specials are not to be missed and represent the best of New England cuisine. There's Yankee pot roast on Mondays, turkey pot pie and American chop suey on Wednesdays, and New England boiled dinner on Thursdays.

And don't forget the pie!

1885 Atlantic Hwy., Waldoboro, 207-832-7785
moodysdiner.com

Moody's still rents a number of cabins seasonally just up the hill from the diner. And they've added a nice little ice cream stand in their expanded parking lot.

WASSES HOT DOGS

"More than five million sold"

Back in 1972, college student Keith Wass purchased a modest hot dog wagon in downtown Rockland from his wife's uncle and spent summer vacation running it. His intention was to work there during summers only while finishing college, but he liked it so much and did so well that he put college on hold and made the hot dog stand his main gig.

Flash forward 50 years, and the stand that bears his name has been a Rockland mainstay ever since Wass took it over. There have been as many as five Wasses stands in Midcoast Maine, and currently there are three. The original 8-by-12-foot hot dog wagon was succeeded in 1986 by Wasses' first bricks-and-mortar location, when Wass purchased a sliver of property at the corner of Main and North Main streets at the bend in Route 1.

The "Wasses" name came about pretty much by accident when one of Keith's suppliers asked what the yet-to-be-named hot dog stand would be called. Keith replied "Wass's Wagon," and the supplier put "Wasses Wagon" on the order form, a distinctly Maine way of expressing the possessive form. Wass was amused and decided to go with "Wasses" for the name.

Enough about history. On to the most salient thing about Wasses: its unique way of making hot dogs. Keith came up with the idea of pouring a thin pool of peanut oil on the griddle, heating it up, grilling the hot dogs in the oil, and sauteing finely chopped

Want to be considered a "regular" at Wasses? On your first visit, order "two with everything" and a chocolate milk. It's Wasses's "secret handshake."

Top left: The Wasses dog with everything (left) and a Western Dog (right).

Above left: Wasses flagship stand on North Main Street in Rockland.

Top right: Hot dogs and diced onions in a hot, shimmering pool of peanut oil.

Center right: Wasses order window with the OVER FIVE MILLION SOLD proclamation.

Above right: A kraut dog.

onions on the same surface. The result is an irresistibly unique hot dog served on a perfectly steamed bun. Regular customers know to order the dogs "with everything," which calls for mustard, relish, and onions. They also know that one dog isn't enough. It's best to start with two, and then go back for more, if needed.

The rest of the menu is quite simple. It's just hot dogs with various toppings, including the Western Dog, a local favorite that's topped with bacon, ketchup, fried onions, and baked beans.

Wasses is only open from 11 a.m. to 4 p.m. and is cash-only, so be sure to time your visit so you don't miss out on this wonderful Midcoast Maine treat.

2 North Main St., Rockland, 207-594-4347

CENTRAL PROVISIONS

Small plates, big flavors

Retrofitted into a sturdy, classic 1800s brick warehouse wharf building dating back to the times of the East India Trading Company, Central Provisions blends the historic and the new seamlessly into one of the best dining experiences in Portland.

The warehouse has been many things over the years, including a wine and bitters shop, a barrel top and burlap bags store, and a supplier of blacksmith and woodworking tools before its current incarnation as a world-class restaurant. Great care has been invested in honoring the history and integrity of the building as it was transformed into the eatery it is today.

Chris and Paige Gould are the founding owners of Central Provisions, each bringing extensive Boston-area restaurant experience to their venture. They opened Central Provisions in the winter of 2014 to immediate acclaim, including a James Beard Best New Restaurant nomination in their inaugural year. They've maintained their popularity with locals through innovative interior design and more importantly a lively, unique menu that wows even the most jaded diners.

Step into this historic structure and the first thing you'll notice is the magnificent woodwork, from the original beams above to the lengthy counter in front of the open kitchen and the finely crafted tables and chairs lining the side wall from front to back. Local craftspeople created these loving touches, along with the handsome metal stools lining the counter, a great spot for watching the chefs at work. A staircase toward the back leads down to a barroom that contains additional seating for diners.

Small plate dining is what Central Provisions is all about, and there are some amazing things to choose from. The range of tastes and textures coming from the open kitchen defies succinct description. Raw items include local oysters, bluefin tuna crudo, a

Top left: Spicy beef salad.

Above left: Many small plates are prepped in the open kitchen.

Top center: Many of Central Provision's small plates are appropriate for carry-out.

Above center: Seats with a kitchen view and tables along the wall.

Top right: Foie gras parfait.

Above right: The sign out front says it all.

spicy beef salad, and caviars procured from local supplier Browne Trading Company. Soups and salads are also of local origin and vary from an inventive ramp vichyssoise to local beet and asparagus salads.

There's a popular brunch that's served Saturday, Sunday, and Monday featuring buckwheat pancakes, popovers, Japanese-inflected hash browns, shirred eggs, skillet cornbread, and a house scrapple, along with an array of sandwiches and small plates. Reservations are recommended for any meal any day at this great spot that mixes wonderful food with a rustic atmosphere in Portland's most historic neighborhood.

414 Fore St., Portland, 207-805-1085
central-provisions.com

DYSART'S RESTAURANT & TRUCK STOP

An Interstate oasis like no other

Dysart's Restaurant & Truck Stop sits just off I-95 on the outskirts of metro Bangor, and it's well known in the trucker world as a port in the storm for those traveling between Northern and Southern Maine. It's also beloved by locals and motorists who enjoy a hot cup of coffee and a good slice of pie as well as belt-busting breakfasts, lunches, and dinners.

Dysart's got its start in 1967 when Dave Dysart and his wife, Irene, opened a somewhat modest fueling station for trucks. Since it took 30 minutes to fill truck fuel tanks back then, they thought it would be nice to add a restaurant so truckers could enjoy a hot meal while waiting on their fill-up. Dave modeled the menu on those he knew from Northern Maine lumber camps, where burly men needed lots of calories to toil in the woods.

The restaurant was originally intended for truckers, but locals and tourists began stopping in as word spread about the great comfort food being served. The restaurant and truck stop have grown steadily over the years into a sprawling operation on both sides of the road, with numerous fuel pumps, truck washes, repair facilities, lots of truck and car parking, a large retail store, and of course, the restaurant.

There are two large dining rooms with spacious seating and plenty of chairs and tables to handle crowds of almost any size. The service is swift and friendly, bringing instant relief to the road-weary. An antique truck and the front grille from a Mack truck semi accentuate the road warrior theme and atmosphere of the establishment.

Top left: One of the many rigs typically found in Dysart's spacious parking lots.

Above left: The wall-mounted Mack Truck grill in the dining room.

Top center: Dysart's, a welcome sight for the road-weary.

Above center: Dave's Favorite Hash breakfast platter.

Right: There's special seating for truckers only.

The restaurant is typically open from 6 a.m. to 8 p.m., and breakfast is perhaps the most popular meal. Among the many items to choose from, the most popular is Dave's Favorite Hash, a generous helping of crumbly, flavorful corned beef hash accompanied by two eggs, toast, and home fries.

If you happen to arrive around 11 a.m. or later, the lunch and dinner menu offers an overwhelming array of comfort foods, the most popular being the homemade country-style pot roast, slow-simmered and smothered in homemade gravy. The lobster roll is made using lobster meat fresh-picked in the kitchen. And the home-baked pies are fine any time of day, especially Dysart's pride and joy: blueberry.

530 Colebrook Rd., Hermon, 207-942-4878
dysarts.com

Check out the video on YouTube showing the Dysarts flubbing their lines, "buttery, flaky crust," over and over while taping a commercial. It was spoofed on *Saturday Night Live*.

BARNACLE BILLY'S

Food and fun on Perkins Cove

Perkins Cove occupies an enviable spot in the charming seaside town of Ogunquit. It sports a small harbor of lobster boats, an arching wooden pedestrian bridge over the cove's channel to the sea, and lovely views of the ocean beyond. Straddling the cove on one side is a 60-year-old lobster shack named for its founder, local legend Billy Tower.

"Barnacle Billy," as he was known, was a lobsterman back in 1961 when a friend offered him prime retail space on the cove to open a dine-in-the-rough lobster shack. The enterprise was a success from the get-go. Designed with a spacious, wrap-around deck overlooking the cove and a cozy interior with a gas-jet fireplace for rainy days, Billy's appealed to the well-heeled seasonal clientele coming to Ogunquit from Boston and New York. George Herbert Walker Bush, a seasonal resident of nearby Kennebunkport, was a regular customer for many years, motoring down in his boat and alighting onto the dock with family and friends (and Secret Service) for frequent lobster feasts.

Several traditions have developed over the years at Barnacle Billy's, such as the starched-white polo shirts emblazoned with the Barnacle Billy's logo and white painter pants worn by all employees, the healthy amount of paprika sprinkled on many of the dishes (especially the lobster rolls and chowder), and the bracing rum punch, which is the go-to, must-have, relaxing drink to be enjoyed with any meal.

Upon entering through the front door of Billy's, you'll find a busy order counter to the left, staffed by several uniformed workers ready to take your order. Beyond the counter is the busy kitchen, with yet more workers hustling to get orders ready. The

Left: Billy's Rum Punch.

Top center: Billy's old-fashioned sign over the front door.

Above center: The kitchen crew, ready to take your order.

Right: Two lobsters, ready for pickup.

menu is posted on a wall next to the counter, revealing all that Billy's has to offer.

Whole boiled lobster is the star of the show and is served with drawn butter. Steamed clams and milky, Maine-style clam chowder are popular starters. The paprika-dusted lobster roll is also very popular—it's a cold roll made with lobster meat, a bit of mayo, and a dash of chopped celery. There's also a fine rotisserie half-chicken.

The Tower family opened a full-service, year-round restaurant next door and gave it the name "Barnacle Billy's etc." It's a more formal alternative to the shack and has a similar lobster-centric menu supplemented with several finned-fish and steak offerings.

70 Perkins Cove Rd., Ogunquit, 207-646-5575
barnbilly.com

Valet parking at a lobster shack? It's a necessity here, with the limited public parking in Perkins Cove. The valet lot across the street from the shack is pricey but well worth it.

HELEN'S RESTAURANT

A Downeast institution with great pie

Helen's and Machias are one in the same in the minds of many, that's how influential the longtime restaurant is in this tight-knit community way up Route 1 in Downeast Maine. Nearly everyone who lives in the town has worked, or knows someone who has worked, at the landmark eatery, which typically employs 40 to 50 people at any time. And if you mention Helen's to the locals, the summer residents, or even to tourists who pass through town, the first thing they'll say in response is "Great pie!"

Helen's first opened its doors in 1950 on Main Street in Machias. Founding owners Helen and Larry Mugnai owned and ran Helen's until 1976, and then sold it to locals Bob and Jean Carter, who moved the restaurant down Main Street to its current location by the Machias River in 1983. They eventually sold Helen's to Jean's sister and her husband, who owned it for the next 20 years.

The current owners, Dave and Julie Barker, first met while working at Helen's in its original Main Street location in the early 1980s. Dave was a dishwasher, and Julie was a server. The couple purchased the restaurant in 2008 and have been the owners ever since.

Helen's burned to the ground in the summer of 2014, but the Barkers rebuilt on the same spot and miraculously reopened the following spring. The restaurant looks pretty much the same on the outside, but the interior features a new, bright, well-lit space with lots of beautifully crafted wood counters and tables and an expansive deck overlooking the river.

The Barkers have kept the menu quite similar to the way it's been for many years while adding a bunch of healthy options, such as broiled haddock in addition to the fried version and a wonderful, locally procured goat cheese salad. Helen's was farm-to-table long

Top left: A display case with tempting pie offerings.

Above left: A slice of Helen's award-winning blueberry pie.

Center: Helen's and Old Glory on a windy day.

Top right: A collection of boxes from old blueberry farms in the area appears in the lobby.

Above right: Helen's beautifully crafted bar.

before it was fashionable, getting produce and meats from local farmers and their seafood from local fishing operations. The starters and entrees are dominated by seafood, and with good reason: the nearby Gulf of Maine offers an abundance of fresh fare.

Then there's the pie—some 10 different types, all made with Helen's famous homemade crust. As Machias sits in the midst of wild blueberry country, the blueberry pie is renowned, especially during harvest season in late summer. But strawberry has for many years been the most popular among blueberry-weary locals who love the red berry almost as much as their native blue.

111 Main St., Machias, 207-255-8423
helensrestaurantmachias.com

In 2010, *Life* magazine named Helen's blueberry pie the best in America.

HARRASEEKET LUNCH AND LOBSTER

Hard to find, tough to beat

Harborside dining is one of the great pleasures to be enjoyed in Maine, and Harraseeket Lunch and Lobster is one of the best places to do it. Off the beaten path and a bit hard to find, Harraseeket (pronounced harrah-SEE-kit) has been feeding locals and tourists alike since 1970. Located right on the harbor in South Freeport just a couple of miles from L. L. Bean, Harraseeket boasts its own fleet of lobster boats in addition to the great seafood it serves up. You'll probably see boats offloading their catch while you're there, guaranteeing any lobster you have will be as fresh as can be.

There are actually three parts to Harraseeket: the seafood shack for deep-fried goodies and sandwiches; the ice cream window, where you order your favorite flavor along with home-baked desserts; and the lobster pound, which has its own order window around the corner from the other two. It's your place for lobsters, clams, potatoes, and corn.

Regis Coffin and her onetime-husband, John, bought a shed on the South Freeport dock in 1970 and began using it as a place to offload John's lobster catch. They started cooking up some of the catch on the dock and selling it to locals for takeaway, eventually adding a few picnic tables for those who wanted to stick around and enjoy their lobsters while taking in the scenic harbor view. Things moved quickly after that, with Regis adding deep fryers and baking ovens and building out a large kitchen, a small enclosed dining room, and an expansive shaded patio out front.

Should you desire deep-fried seafood or sandwiches, step up to the main order window. Menu highlights include fried clams

Left: Harraseeket's hefty whoopie pie.

Top center: Harraseeket's meaty lobster roll.

Above center: Some of Harraseeket's nautical decor.

Top right: Harraseeket Lunch and Lobster on a busy summer day.

Above right: The lobster pound portion of Harraseeket.

(breaded or battered—they're done both ways); lobster rolls (chilled lobster meat on a split-top bun with or without mayo); and a killer fresh fish sandwich on a toasted bun.

If it's boiled or steamed seafood you desire, step around the corner from the main order window and behold the lobster pound and its enticing, wall-mounted menu. Here you may select from whole lobster, steamed clams, crabs, and boiled red potatoes. The pound opens at 7 a.m. every day in season for those who wish to purchase live lobsters for cooking at home.

Lastly, there are the desserts, including ice cream and Harraseeket's famous homemade whoopie pies. Be sure to save room for these unique goodies. No one leaves here hungry.

36 North Main St., South Freeport, 207-865-3535
harraseeketlunchandlobster.com

HARBOR FISH MARKET

New England's premier seafood market

Hidden away on a narrow side-street running the length of Portland's Custom House Wharf, Harbor Fish Market has been plying its trade in the shadows of touristy Commercial Street for over 50 years. The wharf is a throwback to the days when the Portland waterfront was solely the provenance of fishermen, sailors, and stevedores working the docks and moving fish and freight. Harbor Fish offers a wonderful glimpse into the waterfront life of yore—and dishes up some amazing seafood to boot.

There has been a seafood market at Harbor Fish's location ever since the early 1800s. With boat docks in back, it's in the perfect spot to peddle the freshest of seafood. In 1966, brothers Ben Alfiero Sr. and John Alfiero bought the market and proceeded to build its reputation as the best place in the city to go for live lobsters and fresh fish and shellfish. John sold out his share to Ben in 1975, and Ben's sons, Nick, Ben Jr., and Mike, each joined the business as they came of age.

Nick and Mike are still running things, and they've done an amazing job of keeping the market's Old World charm—wood clapboard exterior, concrete floors, iced-down whole fish on display, bushel baskets of oysters—while expanding the business's reach to a worldwide market. At any given time, there are several buyers on the phones in Harbor Fish's back office who are procuring seafood from around the world and matching it with hundreds of wholesale and retail customers.

The Alfieros have produced a wonderful cookbook compendium of their family's recipes, *Harbor Fish Market*, which is for sale in their store.

Left: Customers may hand-pick oysters from icy bins.

Top center: Fresh seafood for home and "away."

Above center: Harbor Fish's vintage storefront.

Right: Locally harvested scallops are one of many specialties.

The store itself is a throwback and a real treat for anyone who loves seafood. Enter through the wooden front door and straight ahead is some 50 linear feet of gleaming glass cases packed with freshly filleted and shucked seafood of every variety. Cod, haddock, pollock, flounder, and numerous other local species are filleted fresh daily by the skilled workers who may be seen through glass in the room behind the counter. Fresh whole fish are displayed on several tables, resting on beds of crushed ice. Oysters and clams may be handpicked by customers from bushels on more tables. And there are several aquamarine-colored cold-water tanks brimming with live lobsters dropped off daily on the wharves out back.

The Alfieros engender a family spirit among their employees and themselves, and their motto is: "We don't sell anything we wouldn't bring home ourselves." That's an assuring commitment that loyal, faithful customers have come to rely on over the years. There's no better place in Maine to experience the freshest and most varied seafood on the market.

9 Custom House Wharf, Portland, 207-775-0251
harborfish.com

FIVE ISLANDS LOBSTER COMPANY

The best lobster shack in the state

Blessed with gorgeous views of Sheepscot Bay and the five islands sitting just offshore, Five Islands Lobster Co. is what everyone dreams of when seeking out the quintessential Maine lobster shack.

The restaurant sits on Georgetown's town dock at the end of Route 127 about a dozen miles south of Bath. In fact, the road dead-ends at Five Islands' front door. The dock is shared with local fishermen, mostly those who fish for lobster, providing a lively and informative backdrop to the Five Islands dining experience.

The Longbottom family has been leasing Five Islands Lobster from the town since 2007, and they've done an excellent job keeping the place running in tip-top shape. There are actually three shacks on the dock: the fry shack, lobster shack, and the ice cream stand.

The first shack encountered is the fry shack, housed in the largest building on the dock. Here you may place your orders for fried seafoods, lobster rolls, burgers and hot dogs, sandwiches, chowders, and soft drinks. (Five Islands is BYO for alcohol.)

For whole lobster, proceed to the lobster shack in back of the fry shack, and queue up to place your order for some of the best lobster in the world. The waters of Sheepscot Bay are some of the deepest and coldest on the Maine coast, propagating a large, healthy lobster population. In this shack, you may choose between hard-shell and soft-shell lobster of varying sizes, and you may elect to have an ear of corn or some red potatoes added to the netted sack with your lobster prior to cooking. Steamer clams and broth are also available here, as is homemade coleslaw. Order your

Left: Five Islands's famed lobster roll.

Top center: The Five Islands fry shack, front and center on the dock.

Above center: The pickup window where you receive your goodies.

Top right: Five Islands Lobster: "Home of the Big Boys."

Above right: The dock is a great place to enjoy your repast.

lobsters first before ordering anything from the fry shack, as the lobsters take longer to cook.

Enjoy your feast at any of the bright green picnic tables on and around the dock. You may watch lobster boats delivering their catch, loading up with bait, and the occasional tuna boat dropping off its landed quarry.

If you've still got room, grab some ice cream from the third shack on the dock. You may choose between cups, cones, and fresh-packed pints for takeaway. Five Islands is your one-stop source for all things lobster, and it should be on everyone's list of must-visits when in Midcoast Maine.

1447 Five Islands Rd., Georgetown, 207-371-2990
fiveislandslobster.com

The fry shack is named the Lovenest Grill, as it's where fishermen of yore used to meet with their girlfriends before returning home from a day at sea.

JORDAN'S SNACK BAR

A multifaceted fun spot with food, cars, games, and country music

Jordan's is like a theme park in miniature, with its food concessions, games arcade, kiddie playground, live country music, and weekly vintage car gatherings, all on two and a half acres along Route 1 as it winds its way toward Downeast Maine. This place has a history going back over 40 years and is a beloved institution to the people of Ellsworth as well as to the thousands of travelers who routinely stop by for a meal or a cone or some live entertainment.

James (Jimmy) Jordan had been working in the family trades of seasonal blueberry raking and tree cultivation when he and his wife, Carol, hit upon the idea of buying into a snack stand on the busy Route 1 on the edge of Ellsworth. Starting with just the food operation in 1981, the Jordans started buying adjacent parcels within a few years, where they constructed an indoor dining and banquets building, an open-air music venue with a dance floor, a small games arcade building, and lots of parking space. Weekly car rallies started soon after and continue to this day in the summer months.

Food is the main focus at Jordan's, and it comes in the form of grilled, deep-fried, and scooped varieties of sandwiches, seafood, and ice cream treats. Burgers are the most popular sandwich item, with several different types to choose from, including the massive Big Jim Triple Burger and the Bacon Cheeseburger.

Wednesdays are Cruise-in Nights in July and August, when locals show up with their vintage rides, a country band plays in the pavilion, and couples dance the night away.

Top left: Jordan's looking much the same as it has for decades.

Above left: Decisions, decisions, decisions.

Top center: A whole-belly fried clam roll.

Above center: The outdoor music pavilion.

Right: Jordan's iconic soft-serve cone sign.

Locally sourced seafood is breaded and fried in Jordan's impressive line of deep fryers, which are kept busy throughout the day. The fried whole-belly clams are the top seller, along with fried haddock, and there's a tasty, chilled lobster roll. Hand-cut onion rings are the side of choice. Hard-packed and soft-serve ice cream are both available and may be ordered by the scoop or as a sundae or banana boat. Jordan's milk shakes are legendary.

Three generations of the Jordan family worked here over the decades until the family finally sold the business to Scott and Katie Kenny in 2017. The Kennys were living in Southern Maine, but Scott has roots in Ellsworth, having attended the local high school. The Kennys have kept the menu pretty much the same as the one established by the Jordans, much to the happiness of regular customers. Here's hoping this roadside fun spot keeps the good times rolling for many years to come.

200 Downeast Hwy., Ellsworth, 207-667-2174
jordanssnackbar.com

EVENTIDE OYSTER CO.

Excellent bivalves and a most unusual lobster roll

Eventide began its life as an offshoot of famed Portland restaurant Hugo's. Co-owners Arlin Smith, Andrew Taylor, and Mike Wiley, young men with culinary chops and lots of ideas to enhance the Portland food scene, bought Hugo's in 2012 and opened Eventide Oyster Co. next door at right about the same time.

Guided by a vision to create an old-fashioned oyster bar with some contemporary twists, Eventide opened to great acclaim and has been a local and tourist favorite ever since. The oyster bar itself consists of a massive block of granite, upon which as many as 20 different types of oysters are on icy display and waiting to be shucked. Stools wrap around the bulky bar and are much coveted and often hard to get. Fear not, however, as there's a string of some 15 additional stools lining the front windows, offering great views of Middle Street. There are also several picnic tables for groups and outdoor café seating in season.

Eventide is housed in a two-story, brick storefront building, sandwiched between Honeypaw (a pan-Asian eatery, the owners' latest restaurant venture) and the currently shuttered Hugo's. Eventide's storefront features floor-to-ceiling glass, allowing lots of natural light to get in, and the color palette within is soft and soothing.

Some of the local Maine oysters featured regularly on the menu include Pemaquid, Winter Point, North Haven, and Glidden Point varieties along with a short list of "imports" from nearby states and overseas origins. Cocktail sauce and a red wine mignonette are the two most popular accompaniments to these pearls of the sea. Littleneck clams and Maine crab claws are also available from the raw bar.

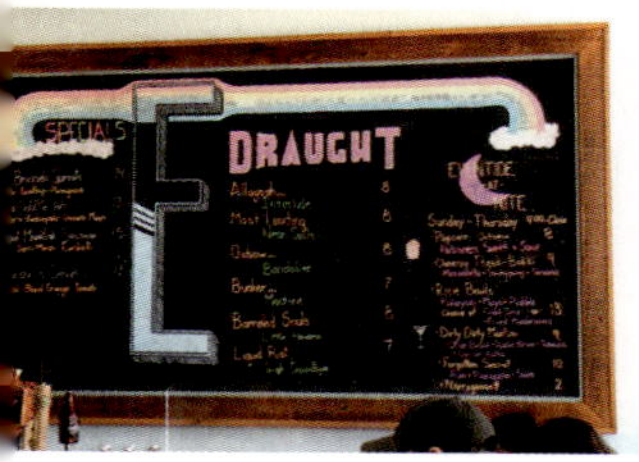

Top left: A dozen oysters on the half shell.

Above left: Special drinks, draughts, and snacks change almost daily.

Center: Café dining on Middle Street.

Top right: The bistro's massive granite oyster bar.

Above right: Eventide's famed Brown Butter Lobster Roll.

The real star of the menu, however, is an unusual take on the Maine lobster roll. The Eventide Brown Butter Lobster Roll is a somewhat miniature version of a regular lobster roll with a couple of important twists: the lobster meat is gently warmed in a brown butter vinaigrette, and it's served on a fluffy, steamed Asian-style bun. The result is a wonderfully tasty combination of flavors and textures that bring the essence of the lobster to life.

Mike Wiley recently stepped away from the business, but Eventide and its sister eateries continue on their steady, successful course. This little stretch of Middle Street in the Old Port offers endless options for unique dining experiences, and Eventide is an important part of that equation.

86 Middle St., Portland, 207-774-8538
eventideoysterco.com

Eventide's famous brown butter lobster roll may be mail-ordered in the form of a kit and shipped anywhere in the country.

APPALACHIAN TRAIL CAFÉ

A must-stop for AT hikers after the over 2,000-mile challenge

Northbound thru-hikers (folks who walk the entire length of the Appalachian Trail) come off Mount Katahdin at the northern terminus of the trail understandably famished, and many make a beeline for the best breakfast and lunch place in nearby Millinocket: the Appalachian Trail Café.

Housed in a quaint storefront on a narrow, one-way street in the downtown area, this eatery has become legendary among hikers, visitors to Baxter State Park, and loyal locals who come for the great food and the trail stories being told by those who have gone the distance.

Covid nearly forced the permanent closure of this longstanding institution in 2020, but longtime waitress and local preschool teacher Leah Malcolm came to the rescue, buying the place and reopening it in the summer of 2021. She says she did it because she loves the customers. It's housed in one of the oldest buildings on Millinocket's Penobscot Avenue, and everyone's thrilled that the café carries on.

Tots (as in Tater Tots) play a major role in the café's breakfast offerings. Think of it this way: there are no home-fried potatoes at breakfast but an abundance of tots, which come with just about every dish.

The Millinocket Special, one of the café's most popular dishes, consists of chopped tots mixed with grilled onions and melted cheddar cheese. Another interesting tot creation is the Veggie Tots plate. This time, the tots are served with grilled onions, bell peppers, fresh spinach, mushrooms, diced tomatoes, and cheddar cheese. Tots also accompany many of the other dishes, such as the Tot

Left: The Appalachian Trail Café on Penobscot Avenue.

Center: The Veggie Tots plate.

Top right: Appalachian Trail Café mugs for sale.

Above right: The cozy counter for coffee and more.

Poutine platter, where the potato cylinders take the place of french fries, and cheddar cheese stands in for curds.

A longstanding café tradition is thru-hikers signing the ceiling tiles suspended in the dining room. The prefab rectangles contain thousands of signatures and short notes, with most contributors signing their "trail names," monikers they adopt during their long journey from Georgia to Maine. (The tiles are now full, and future signees are being directed down to the Trail Lodge, where the tradition continues.)

Whether or not you hike the trail or visit the park, check this place out for some good food and great stories.

210 Penobscot Ave., Millinocket, 207-723-6720

BEAL'S LOBSTER PIER

A kaleidoscopic selection of lobster rolls and more

Beal's celebrated its 90th anniversary in 2022, a testament to the staying power and appeal of this working lobster pier and acclaimed seafood shack. Located on its own wharf next to the Coast Guard station in Southwest Harbor, Beal's features lobster fresh off the boat and so much more.

Founded by H. R. Beal as a pier for lobstermen in 1932, Beal's began as a lobster wholesaling business, an activity that continues to this day. The restaurant opened on the pier in 1969 when Suzanne Beal and her sister-in-law began selling lobster rolls at the foot of the dock. Suzanne's father decided to open a full-fledged seafood shack on the pier in the 1980s, and the restaurant and pier remained in the Beal family until 2014, when it was purchased by Stu Snyder and his business partner. Three generations of Beals established the patterns of success for the wholesaling and restaurant operations, and Snyder is faithfully continuing those fine traditions.

Beal's today is a busy place from May through October, with hundreds of customers flocking to the open-air restaurant every day. In addition to the picnic tables scattered along the foot of the pier, there's an enclosed dining area with windows overlooking the harbor. The big double doors that mark the restaurant's entrance are nearly always open throughout the summer, as customers queue up and study the voluminous chalkboard menu suspended behind the order counter. There's also a cold-water tank right by the entrance where you may select your own lobster and have it weighed on the spot.

Whole boiled lobster is de rigueur for this place, but there are many other delectable comestibles to consider. When Snyder

Top left: Fresh-caught lobsters being off-loaded on the dock.

Above left: Beal's wide-open, friendly entrance.

Top center: There's plenty of food and drink to choose from.

Above center: Beal's classic lobster roll.

Right: Beal's list of lobster roll varieties.

took ownership, he rolled out half a dozen different types of lobster rolls, all served on brioche buns. There are cold and hot versions as well as one served with garlic butter, a spicy buffalo version, and a lobster roll po' boy with zesty Cajun-style seasoning.

Great starters include steamed mussels or clams and Maine oysters shucked and sold by the dozen. The deep fryers yield great haddock, scallop, and shrimp baskets, and a hefty seafood platter. A full-service bar offers all sorts of libations.

While enjoying your meal on the pier, keep watch for lobster boats pulling in and offloading their catches at the end of the pier. It's visual proof that your lobster is as fresh as can be.

182 Clark Point Rd., Southwest Harbor, 207-244-3202
bealslobster.com

KING EIDER'S PUB

A classic neighborhood pub with great food and drink

This place is the beating heart and soul of downtown Damariscotta. Initially opened in 1996, King Eider's Pub (or just "the pub," as locals refer to it) is where locals have been gathering for more than 25 years to enjoy good food, great beverages, and the comfort and companionship of the local community.

Co-owners Todd and Sarah Maurer and Jed and Cynthia Weiss (the wives are sisters) have been at the helm since 2003. Sarah and Cynthia's sister, Melissa Organ, joined the team in 2010, making it a true family operation. The group was named restaurateurs of the year in 2018 by the Maine Restaurant Association. Their unwavering commitment to outstanding customer service is apparent from the time you arrive until you pay your check and say good-bye.

The pub is reminiscent of those found all over England and Ireland, with whimsical decor and a cozy atmosphere where regulars like to gather and get caught up over a pint and a plate of fish and chips or shepherd's pie. It's housed in a pretty, two-story brick building set a bit off of Main Street with a lovely patio and several tables out front. Climb up a few stairs, enter through the front door, and you're immediately greeted by a gracious host who will help guide you to the best spot in the pub for your needs.

In the summer of 2022, the owners sold the restaurant to two longtime employees, Scott McArdle and Damon Waltz, who are committed to keeping King Eider's Pub the wonderful gathering place that it's been for 20 years.

Left: The pub's classy exterior.

Top center: Nicely seasoned pub fries.

Above center: King Eider's Signature Salad.

Top right: The warm, inviting oyster bar.

Above right: Bangers and mash.

The first floor houses the pub room, beautifully decorated, with tables and several stools at the bar and lots of handmade mugs hanging from the ceiling. There's an extensive list of over 150 whiskeys that may be ordered individually or in flights. (There are a dozen different flights to choose from.) Beers and ales on draft feature a couple from Ireland and half a dozen from local Maine brewers. Bottled and canned brews are numerous, many imported from the British Isles.

Halfway up the staircase to the second-floor dining room is a cozy little oyster bar with a couple of stools at the shucking station. The oysters are harvested locally and purchased directly from Damariscotta River oyster farmers.

Menu highlights for lunch and dinner include hand-cut pub fries seasoned with a dry rub, a grilled salmon salad, and standout pub favorites such as steak and ale pie, bangers and mash, and of course, fish and chips.

Seek out this fine spot for great food, fine spirits, and a warm atmosphere whenever you're in Midcoast Maine. It's a year-round delight.

12 Elm St., Damariscotta, 207-563-6008
kingeiderspub.com

BAYLEY'S LOBSTER POUND

Home of Maine's original lobster roll

Bayley's Lobster Pound, in the Pine Point section of Scarborough, celebrated its 100th anniversary in 2015. It's the oldest continuously operating lobster pound in the state. In addition to its thriving lobster wholesaling business, Bayley's has a wonderful seafood market and a full-service restaurant (the Bait Shed) for seafood lovers to get their fix of lobsters and much more.

The story began when Stephen and Ella Bayley relocated to Pine Point from Wells, Maine, in 1915 so that Stephen could begin working at the large Snow clam-processing plant in Pine Point. Bayley supplemented his income by digging clams on the nearby flats and fishing the coastal waters with lobster pots. Ella cooked up the catch, and after a while, she started selling some of the excess lobster catch through her kitchen window to neighbors and friends.

Lobstering eventually became a full-time pursuit for the Bayleys, with Stephen and his then partner selling to local restaurants and seafood markets. They became known for taking some of their fresh-caught, unsold lobsters, putting them in suitcases, packing them with seaweed, and then hopping on the local train to Portland and selling them in the city's markets.

Flash forward to today, and Bayley's is a warehouse-sized operation currently owned and run by fourth-generation family member Susan (Bayley) Clough and her husband, Vincent. Much of the floor space in Bayley's big building is taken up with lobster tanks and seafood processing for the wholesale market, but there's an excellent retail seafood market that can handle all your seafood needs.

Bayley's also makes a great lobster roll, which may be purchased over the counter and enjoyed on benches and chairs outside the market. The Bayley family claims to have invented the

Top left: The Bait Shed's long pier is a great place to dine.

Above left: A fresh shipment of locally sourced steamer clams.

Center: Bayley's will cook your lobster for you to take home.

Top right: Freshly filleted fish in the seafood market.

Above right: The sign pointing to the lobster pound and Bait Shed restaurant.

Maine lobster roll back in the day when Stephen would ask Bella to make him lobster sandwiches on white bread with the crusts cut off. Bella tired of trimming the crusts, so she started stuffing the lobster into top-split hot dog buns. Voila!

Whole lobsters abound in the pound's open-air lobster tanks, where you may select your own and even have it cooked on the premises for takeaway. This one-stop seafood emporium should be all you need to get your seafood fix in this pretty part of Maine.

9 Avenue 6, Scarborough, 207-883-4571
bayleys.com

In 2012, Bayley's added a bar and seafood restaurant, the Bait Shed, adjacent to the pound on their lengthy L-shaped dock, which extends into the scenic Nonesuch River.

LUNCH ON THE WHARF

A little gem on the Downeast shore

It's a bit of a chore finding your way to Corea, Maine, and Lunch on the Wharf, but it's well worth the effort if you're a fan of fresh seafood (especially lobster) and if you love to watch the goings-on of a real working harbor.

This lunch spot (it's only open 11 a.m. to 3 p.m.) got its start as an art gallery of sorts named Corea Wharf Gallery. Local lobsterman Joe Young opened the small venue in his former bait shed, which he painted white on the inside to make a suitable place to hang artwork. His primary goal was to showcase the photography of his late aunt, who spent years documenting life in and around Corea Harbor.

In order to attract more people to the gallery, Young's wife suggested he sell some food on the wharf. Their son was commissioned to set up a hot dog cart, which expanded to selling Italian sausage sandwiches, and then eventually lobster rolls. People started showing up for the food and hanging around to check out the art. The name was changed to Wharf Gallery and Grill. Young procured a trailer and converted it into a kitchen, and plenty of picnic tables and other seating were added to the wharf.

Flash forward to today, and Lunch on the Wharf is now solely a food service operation with a reputation that pulls in customers from Maine and beyond. The pothole-riddled parking lot is filled with cars bearing license plates from all over the country, surprising given the obscure location of the place.

Step onto the wharf and study the menu on a whiteboard. There's plenty to choose from, including starter specials such as stuffed clams and locally harvested oysters on the half shell. The haddock chowder and clam chowder are made fresh daily on the

Left: Open-air dining on the wharf.

Top center: Lunch on the Wharf's partially hidden shack.

Above center: Lobster grilled cheese.

Right: Shed and traps on an adjacent wharf.

dock, and there's a gas-fired lobster cooker on full display next to the menu board. Lobster rolls and lobster grilled cheese are the most popular sandwiches, and the hot dog and Italian sausage have retained their place on the menu.

Then there's the boiled lobster, fresh out of the cooker and served with two sides and a beverage. (The wharf is BYOB, by the way.) Be sure to order before 2 p.m., as the workers like to clear out by 3 p.m. sharp.

The bait shed has been converted into a small, enclosed dining area, but the view of the harbor from the wharf is preferred for anyone seeking some solace by the sea.

13 Gibbs Lane, Corea, 207-963-9077
corealunch.com

SPORTSMAN'S KITCHEN AND KEG

A year-round oasis for outdoors enthusiasts

Sebago Lake is the second largest lake in Maine and also the state's deepest. It's been a magnet for outdoor recreationists for as long as anyone can remember, and its shores are populated with hundreds of cabins, campgrounds, marinas, and beach parks. The lake's southern shore is particularly popular, and that's where you'll find Sportsman's Kitchen and Keg, a relative newcomer to the local dining scene, yet with roots to an old-time Portland bar and grill.

Sportsman's is the brainchild of Paul and Rocco Severino, a father-and-son team with experience and memories that go back to the old Sportsman's Grill on Congress Street in Portland. The 50-year-old restaurant, across from Portland's former Greyhound bus depot, closed in the 1980s. Italian-American dishes were the grill's hallmark. Paul, who was working there at the time with his father and uncles, shifted to a career in insurance, while son, Rocco, began pursuing restaurant jobs around Portland. Several years ago, the two decided to partner in a new restaurant in Sebago, near where the Severino family has vacationed for decades. They bought an existing restaurant with eight rental cottages and put their own stamp on the property, which includes a 90-foot lake dock across the street.

One of the first things you'll likely notice at Sportsman's is the fun, funky, freestanding covered bar in the restaurant's front yard. It has a dozen or so stools wrapped around all four sides, where

There are a dozen or so local beers, ales, and hard ciders available on tap at any given time from Sportsman's indoor bar.

Left: Dine indoors or out at the restaurant.

Top center: The 1/2 fried chicken, with fried brussels sprouts and roasted potatoes.

Above center: Sportsman's is located on Sebago Lake's south shore.

Top right: The fun, airy front yard bar.

Above right: There are a dozen libations on tap in the barroom.

patrons engage in lively conversations while others enjoy yard games like cornhole. It's a great place to chill before or after dining at the restaurant. The lodge-like restaurant has plenty of umbrellaed tables outside and a cozy, wood-paneled dining room and bar within.

Sportsman's menu is an eclectic mix of upscale pub grub and more experimental fare that changes pretty regularly. Crispy fried brussels sprouts with a balsamic glaze is a popular starter, as is the Northwest River Nachos, a massive platter of homemade tortilla chips, melted cheese, vegetables, salsa, and sour cream.

Some of the more interesting entrees harken back to the grill days in Portland, where such pasta dishes as the Gravy (meatballs or sausage over pasta bathed in the Severino's famed red sauce), Severino Scampi (chicken or shrimp covered in garlic, butter, white wine, and spinach), and 909 Congress Street (breaded eggplant or chicken with red sauce, and then baked with mozzarella and parmesan cheeses).

No one leaves hungry, and many take home enough leftovers for the next day's dinner.

46 Sebago Rd., Sebago, 207-787-5209
skksebago.com

FISHERMAN'S CATCH

The lobster shack with a trolley car out front

Looking every bit like the seafood shack that it is, Fisherman's Catch has been a mainstay on the Wells food scene ever since it opened in the early 1980s. It's strategically positioned on the road that leads to Wells Harbor, which has made it a longtime favorite for local boaters. Consisting of a series of low-slung buildings, a wheel-less green trolley car, and a generous outdoor patio overlooking a nearby salt marsh, this place beckons to all those seeking a genuine Maine seafood experience.

The shack began as an offshoot of a small lobster pound owned by the Walters family, who then sold it to the Lane family in the 1990s, who in turn sold it to current owners Nick and Amy Cardinali in 2005. Nick had just graduated from college and was working at a seafood restaurant in Kennebunkport when the shack came up for sale. He took a chance, bought the place, and has been at the helm ever since.

The Cardinalis wisely kept things pretty much as they were when they first bought it, and the locals and returning tourists have repaid them by coming back again and again. Nick is particularly proud of the fact that many of the employees have been around for more than 15 years, a testament to the love the local community feels for the place.

Lobster is the main show here, and, as is the case with many shacks, lobster rolls are the most popular item. Served in the traditional Maine style of chilled lobster meat mixed with a bit of mayo, and then served on a leaf of lettuce tucked into a toasted bun, it's a fine roll on its own. However, if you're feeling adventurous, you may add crumbled bacon, drawn butter, or a lemon truffle aioli to the mix for slight upcharges. Whole lobster

Top left: The meaty lobster roll.

Above left: A roadside view of Fisherman's Catch.

Center: A well-weathered sign bearing the Fisherman's Catch logo.

Right: Fisherman's Catch's airy indoor dining room.

dinners include single or twin steamed lobsters accompanied by chips, homemade coleslaw, and a dinner roll.

Deep-fried seafood is breaded and cooked in super-clean oil. There are several tempting combo platters, particularly the Captain's Feast, a mountain of deep-fried goodness definitely enough for two or more.

The trolley used to ply the streets, transporting tourists during the busy summer season. Now it serves as a staging area for food, libations, and a small bar area. There's live music almost nightly from mid-June through Labor Day. And the marsh provides glimpses of local wildlife.

134 Harbor Rd., Wells, 207-646-8780
fishermanscatchwells.com

Rolls of paper towels hang suspended from the rafters above each table in the dining room, making for quick and easy cleanup after feasting on whole lobsters and more.

PALACE DINER

Contemporary takes on classic diner fare

This Pollard diner car, one of only two still in existence, has a long and storied history of serving hot meals to the workers of Biddeford, Maine. Biddeford is an historic Saco River mill town that is in the process of reinventing itself as a hipster haven with trendy restaurants, upscale shops, and incubator business start-ups, many of which are located in the handsome, refurbished red brick buildings that for many decades housed Biddeford's textile mills.

The Palace story began in Lowell, Massachusetts, where the Palace Diner car rolled off the Pollard Diner Car Company's assembly line in 1927 and then was shipped to downtown Biddeford, where it has been ever since. Diner aficionados love its distinct architectural features, many of which have survived through the ages quite nicely. The 15 stools, well-worn countertop, tile floor, barrel-roofed ceiling, and chrome backsplashes are just some of the highlights of this throwback gem.

The diner has been owned by a number of families over the years, starting with the four-decade run of Louis LaChance, a French-Canadian transplant eager to serve familiar fare to his fellow expats working in the busy mills. Many diners got their starts feeding factory workers, and the Palace is no exception. A popular and enduring dish here is poutine, a Canadian dish consisting of grilled home fries and melted cheddar cheese curds smothered in homemade beef gravy—hearty fare for hard-working folks often putting in six days of labor a week.

Be sure to check out the LADIES INVITED signs gracing the diner's façade. Back in the day, it was considered unladylike to sit on stools in eateries, hence the special appeal to hesitant women.

Left: The diner's barrel-roofed interior.

Top center: The Palace Diner's distinctive red façade has graced the streets of Biddeford since 1927.

Above center: The Palace Diner's exterior retains its original vintage charm. Courtesy Palace Diner

Right: The Palace's famed fried chicken sandwich.

Four succeeding families owned and ran the diner from 1960 to 2014, when current owners Greg Mitchell and Chad Conley bought the place and turned it on its ear. Introducing a menu that's equal parts diner and hipster fare, the newly invented Palace garnered immediate praise from the press and from the influx of young inhabitants eager to help reinvent the city.

The two most distinctive dishes on the Palace menu these days are the fried chicken sandwich—a massive piece of chicken breast deep fried and topped with cabbage slaw, jalapenos, and mayo and served on a sesame bun with an iceberg lettuce salad on the side—and the internationally acclaimed tuna melt, served on grilled challah bread with pickles, mayo, and iceberg lettuce. These two sandwiches alone have put the cozy diner squarely in the center of America's culinary stage.

Don't miss this one-of-a-kind transformed diner, an eatery that has reinvented itself many times over.

18 Franklin St., Biddeford, 207-284-0015
palacedinerme.com

GURNET TRADING CO.

Excellent seafood from a longtime fishing family

Gurnet Trading Co. is a hands-on operation. Owned by Brian and Julie Soper, this busy couple has caught, cleaned, and cooked virtually all of its seafood offerings through its seafood market and take-out stand since its founding in 2003. The Sopers have been involved in the Maine seafood industry their entire lives, and it shows in the quality of goods they provide through their shack, market, and wholesale businesses.

It's easy to spot Gurnet Trading Co. when you're cruising down Gurnet Road in Brunswick heading south toward Harpswell. It's housed in a one-story, grey-shingled, blue-trimmed building hard by the road and surrounded by sheltering trees. It looks like something you'd expect to see in the Pacific Northwest, cozy and quaint and nestled in the forest, yet it contains some of the best Maine seafood in the area.

Gurnet's site actually used to be a junkyard, filled with old cars and machinery. Brian and Julie bought the property, much to the consternation of their families, and they proceeded to clean it up and get it ready for retail. Brian has been a longtime scallop diver, and he continues to participate with his team during the winter season. During the summer, the Sopers may be found cooking and cleaning in their kitchen where they and their staff pick all their own lobster and crab meat and shuck all their own clams. The fish fillets come from carefully selected local cutters.

There's a menu and an order window on the front of the shack for carryout orders. Chowders and stews are outstanding, especially the milk-based, Maine-style seafood chowder, chockful of lobster, shrimp, scallops, and haddock. Another standout is the thick, creamy lobster stew.

Left: Some of Brian Soper's famed diver scallops.

Above left: Gurnet's woodsy look and feel.

Center: "No Face," who has lost his wooden visage to Mother Nature over the years.

Right: A cup of the rich, flavorful seafood chowder.

Above right: A bit of whimsy in Gurnet's seafood market.

On the deep-fried side, Brian's "Dive" scallops are the most interesting and rewarding choice—sea scallops plucked fresh from the bottom of Casco Bay. The lobster roll is generously portioned with fresh meat mixed with a bit of mayo and served on a toasted bun. Though the limited indoor seating is no longer available, there are a couple of tables out front for al fresco dining and several picnic tables overlooking the creek running in back of the shack.

The seafood market has taken over the shack's interior, and there is no fresher seafood to be found anywhere in the Brunswick area. Make this your go-to place to grab some seafood (including live lobsters) for cooking at home.

602 Gurnet Rd., Brunswick, 207-729-7300
gurnettrading.com

SEA BASKET

Deep-fried seafood at its best

While Red's Eats and Sprague's Lobster battle it out for best lobster roll in Wiscasset, there's no contest in this river town when it comes to deep fried seafood. The winner is the Sea Basket, a somewhat unassuming, whitewashed eatery in a handsome building on Route 1 a mile west of the two lobster emporiums.

Initially opened in 1956, the Sea Basket started down by the Sheepscot River before moving to its current location on Route 1. The Belanger family purchased it in 1981 and made the move, though it was significantly smaller than it is now. The Belangers sold it to Jimmy Asprogiannis, who brought on college friend John Toumanides to help him run the place. Dining rooms were added to both sides of the small shack, greatly expanding its capacity and allowing for nearly year-round dining.

In 2017, the restaurant changed hands once again, when Louis Rylant, a New Hampshire car dealership owner and sometime restaurateur, snapped up the Sea Basket and kept Toumanides on as general manager, a post he still holds today. Throughout the ownership changes, the Sea Basket has maintained its exceptional commitment to quality when it comes to its menu, especially its deep-fried offerings. Rylant added a lovely patio with umbrellaed tables to one side of the building, a prescient move in light of the adjustments necessitated during the initial waves of Covid-19.

Today, the Sea Basket is a joy inside and out. The walls are decorated with floor-to-ceiling, duo-toned images of the Wiscasset

The haddock chowder, seafood stew, clam chowder, and famed lobster stew are all available in frozen pints for takeaway and enjoyment at home.

Left: The Sea Basket's clean, whitewashed look.
Top center: The massive haddock sandwich and fried potato wedges.
Above center: A heaping helping of deep-fried, whole-belly clams.
Right: The Sea Basket's nicely appointed interior.

waterfront from days gone by. There are plenty of spacious booths and tables spread out over three rooms, and the patio provides great al fresco dining.

A few Pitco fryers form the heart of the cooking operation and keep the kitchen humming. Canola oil is used exclusively in them and is routinely filtered several times each day. The clams come from local Maine clam beds, and the lobster meat is supplied exclusively by Atlantic Edge in nearby Boothbay, a longtime Sea Basket supplier.

Fried clams are the most popular item from the deep fryers. Breaded fresh haddock, scallops, and clam strips all come in platters, baskets, or solo. The much-lauded lobster stew has made national news multiple times. And yes, there is a lobster roll, available in four-ounce and half-pound sizes.

The Sea Basket adds variety to the seafood dining scene in Wiscasset and should be considered a great alternative to the lobster roll competition on the town's waterfront.

303 Bath Rd., Wiscasset, 207-882-6581
seabasket.com

SUSAN'S FISH-N-CHIPS

Great deep-fried seafood—and free coffee

For some of the best deep-fried seafood in Portland, you have to head inland a few miles from downtown to a seafood shack that shares a cinder block building with an automobile radiator shop. Susan's Fish-n-Chips has been serving up quality, deep-fried seafood from here for more than 30 years, and owner Susan Ekland has been at the helm the entire time.

This one-of-a-kind eatery has no pretensions of being a hip spot trying to look retro or industrial. Susan's is the real deal, popular with locals who don't bat an eye when they enter the cavernous, garage-like space with high ceilings and tons of nautical kitsch hanging from the walls and ceiling. The space was clearly once occupied by some sort of automotive service business, with its roll-up, glass-windowed bay doors and ceiling-mounted fluorescent light fixtures. Picnic tables are scattered throughout, there are several seats at the counter, and a small patio area out back.

Susan has been known to roll out all sorts of unusual deals for the benefit of her customers, including free coffee every day from a pot by the order counter. She also doesn't weigh out each portion of lobster for her popular lobster roll, preferring instead to eyeball it and heap it on.

Deep-fried seafood is the main draw here, with the namesake fish and chips leading the parade. It features a few perfectly breaded and fried squares of haddock accompanied by fries and homemade coleslaw. The breading station and fryers are just over the counter in full view for curious customers. Along with fish and chips, there are a variety of "dinnahs" featuring various types of fried shellfish, such as clams, clam strips, smelt, scallops, and shrimp. Potato salad or pasta salad may be substituted for fries.

Top left: A plate of Susan's namesake fish and chips.

Above left: Susan's shares a building with a radiator repair shop.

Center: All the breading and battering take place in full view.

Top right: Lunch for four.

Above right: The colorful dining area.

In addition to the popular lobster roll, there's a seasonal special on deep-fried lobster tails, served on a wooden stick and accompanied by a small cup of melted butter.

If you've got room for dessert, try Susan's deep-fried ice cream or the deep-fried banana split with bananas, peanut butter ice cream, hot fudge, whipped cream, and a cherry. It's a meal in itself.

Don't miss this roadside oasis. It's some of the best fried seafood you'll find in Portland.

1135 Forest Ave., Portland, 207-878-3240
susansfishnchips.com

Bring your fresh-caught, cleaned fish to Susan's, and they'll cook it up for you for five dollars per two pounds of fish.

STRESS FREE MOOSE PUB

A northwoods classic

Moosehead Lake in Maine's northwoods is a year-round destination for outdoors enthusiasts, with boating, swimming, and hiking in the summer and ice fishing, hunting, and snowmobiling in winter. And after a day in the great outdoors, there's no better place to let your hair down and blow off a little steam than at Greenville's delightful Stress Free Moose Pub.

This super-friendly neighborhood place first opened in 2003 in a small house on the edge of Greenville's business district. Founders Rich Czopek and Chandra Bardwell ran Stress Free for several years before selling it to the current owner, Stacey Duncan. In the intervening years, Stacey has turned the pub into a festive, multifaceted restaurant and watering hole with live entertainment and themed holiday celebrations throughout the year.

The small house has been remodeled and expanded a couple of times and is now a two-story structure with a rooftop deck and plenty of outdoor seating. The bar and dining area within the house are warm and inviting, with stacked-log wallpaper and a mounted zebra head (tricked out with moose antlers) in the dining room, a lively wraparound bar, and a massive moose head hanging from the wall in a side dining nook. There's a second-floor dining area filled with mismatched tables and chairs and scrawlings all over the walls from patrons.

Interestingly, the menu leans heavily toward seafood, with steamed mussels and a smoked trout plate for appetizers and baked stuffed haddock, grilled salmon, fish and chips, and shrimp or scallop scampi for entrees. Another interesting opener is the Giant Pub Pretzel—soft, chewy, and salty and served with a bowl of beer cheese or spicy pub mustard. The Summer Berry Salad is laden

Left: The Giant Pub Pretzel with beer cheese.

Top center: The Stress Free Moose's rooftop deck and patio tables.

Above center: One of several neon tributes to the "Moose."

Right: A stuffed moose head presides over the dining area and bar.

with strawberries and blueberries on a bed of baby spinach, red onions, and feta cheese.

Fridays and Saturdays feature dinner specials such as sesame-crusted ahi tuna, a crabmeat-stuffed portobello mushroom, braised short ribs, and pan-seared scallops. Lunchtime offers a nice selection of sandwiches like an avocado BLT with applewood smoked bacon, a pastrami Rueben, and a surprisingly good whole-belly clam roll. Numerous local Maine beers are on tap at all times, and the liquor shelf is deep, varied, and well stocked.

Perhaps Stress Free's greatest appeal is its friendly, neighborhood atmosphere and the loyal, long-serving staff Stacey has lovingly cultivated over the years. Walk through the door here, and you immediately feel at home.

65 Pritham Ave., Greenville, 207-695-3100
stressfreemoose.com

Toasted Trivia Tuesday is a longstanding trivia-night tradition at the Stress Free Moose. It's hosted by local personality and frequent Moose habitue, John Hess.

JORDAN POND HOUSE

Tea and popovers in a gorgeous setting

Tea and popovers have been a tradition at this Acadia National Park restaurant almost since its inception as a restaurant in the late 1800s. Today, tens of thousands of visitors stop by this lovely spot to partake of this snack and to soak up the gorgeous scenery surrounding Jordan Pond itself. Before getting to the actual refreshments, let's take a quick look at the history of this beloved homestead by the pond and how it came to be.

Back in the 1840s, the first settlers in the Jordan Pond area established a logging operation and sawmill near the foot of the pond. The Jordan family of nearby Seal Harbor built the original farmhouse structure here. Over the next several decades, the pond became a popular vacation spot for summer visitors. Thomas and Nellie McIntire served the first tea and popovers to guests at Jordan Pond around 1895. John D. Rockefeller purchased the property in 1928 and donated it to the National Park Service. The McIntyres continued to run the restaurant until 1945, all the while serving their tea and popovers along with a brief lunch menu.

The original house, with its birch bark dining rooms and fieldstone fireplaces, burned down in 1979. It was replaced by the current structure in 1982. The indoor dining area boasts high ceilings, a large stone fireplace, floor-to-ceiling windows, and fetching modern light fixtures dangling in an artistic arrangement from the ceiling. Dozens of green benches and tables grace the lawn in back

Be sure to make a priority seating reservation through the Jordan Pond House website prior to your visit, especially in the summertime.

Left: Outdoor benches and tables offer a great place to enjoy the surroundings.
Top center: The Jordan Pond House menu, which tells the story of this historic place.
Above center: A Jordan Pond popover with lemonade.
Top right: The high-ceilinged main dining room.
Above right: The Jordan Pond restaurant, constructed in 1982.

of the house, offering excellent views of the pond and forested hills beyond as well as a great place to enjoy the comestibles.

Jordan Pond offers an enticing menu of locally procured seafoods, greens, and meats. Cheeses and seafood snacks like crab cakes and smoked salmon start things off, followed by seafood and farmer's market chowders and stews.

Then there's the tea and popovers, a grand English tradition that has prevailed here for over 100 years. There's a choice of teas (or lemonades, if you prefer), and the puffy, flaky popovers are served hot, two per order, and accompanied by whipped butter and organic strawberry jam. Many visitors come just for the tea and popovers. Even if you decide to dine indoors, be sure to step outside and behold the splendid view of the pond and mountains forming the backdrop for this idyllic scene.

2928 Park Loop Rd., 207-276-3781
jordanpondhouse.com

FLO'S HOT DOGS

It's all about the relish.

Back in 1959, Florence Stacy (aka "Flo") bought a roadside food stand in Cape Neddick and quickly became legend in the food lore of Maine. This diminutive wooden roadside shack has no phone, no lobster roll or other seafood, and no spare headroom inside. It's only open from 11 a.m. to 3 p.m., and there are often long lines of people waiting to order.

Flo ruled over her namesake eatery until 1973, when she sold it to her son and daughter-in-law, John and Gail Stacy, and they remain owners to this day. Their daughter, Kim, who has worked at Flo's on and off for many years, is next in line, and no changes are planned any time in the future.

The story goes that Flo was a teacher in a one-room schoolhouse in Maine for many years before buying the hot-dog shack more than 60 years ago. Her good-natured sparring with customers was legendary, berating them for ordering improperly, cutting in line, and talking out of turn, among other perceived offenses. Locals and regulars took her belligerence to be part of the charm of the place, though some first-timers cowered in fear or left in indignation upon experiencing Flo's sharp tongue. Gail says Flo sent her home in tears nearly every day for the first four years she worked there. Nonetheless, she persevered, marrying Flo's son and taking over the business.

So, why do locals and hordes of tourists continue to patronize this tiny roadside relic? It's mostly for the hot dogs. The customers'

Flo's hot dogs and buns are steamed in metal boxes, and the ends of the wieners clipped off for unique flavor and presentation.

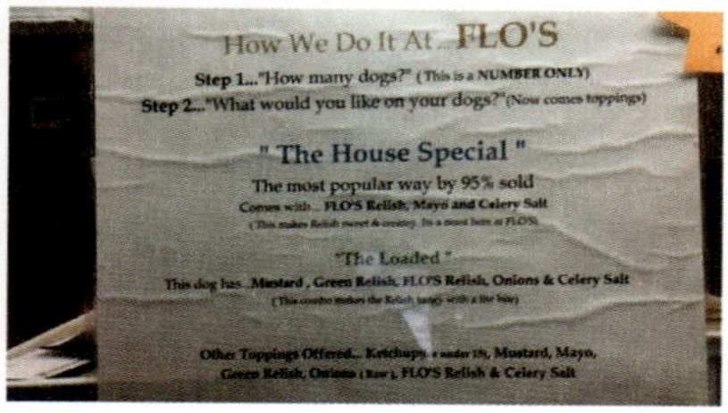

Top left: Flo's simple roadside sign.

Above left: The recently created outdoor order window.

Top right: "The House Special" (left) and the "Loaded" (right).

Center right: Look for the red shack and "Open" flag on Route 1.

Above right: Flo's no-nonsense menu.

favorite is the House Special, a steamed pup adorned with Flo's special relish, mayonnaise, and a dash of celery salt. The "Loaded" dog (second most popular) comes with mustard, green relish, Flo's relish, chopped onions, and celery salt. Moxie soda, in bright orange cans, is the beverage of choice.

The relish is homemade, and its recipe is a closely guarded secret. Dark and smoky in color and flavor, it has become so popular that Flo's now sells it by the jar. There's no indoor seating and a few picnic tables are scattered outside. And there's certainly no shame in wolfing down your wieners while sitting in your car out front. You'll have plenty of company.

1359 Route 1, Cape Neddick
floshotdogs.com

YOUNG'S LOBSTER POUND

Lobster (and more) on a grand scale

If ever you want to get a close-up look at the lobster wholesaling business (and who doesn't?), pay a visit to Young's Lobster Pound near the top of Penobscot Bay, and while you're there, treat yourself to a wonderful lobster dinner in the rough.

Young's doesn't look like your typical lobster shack. It's a two-story, steel-paneled, red-and-white warehouse building on the waterfront in East Belfast. The only things hinting at the seafood to be had within are a sign over the massive front entry advertising shore dinners and the whimsical statue by the door portraying a small bear in Gloucester fishing gear, holding a lobster and bearing the name CAPT. SEAWEED on his lapel.

Step inside and behold dozens of aquamarine-colored saltwater tanks that can hold up to 30,000 lobsters, most of which are sold to seafood processors and to retailers like grocery stores, restaurants, and seafood markets. The tanks are stacked three-high and line both walls leading to the back of the warehouse.

Before wandering too far in, be sure to check out the order counter on the righthand side by the front door, where you may purchase a lobster shore dinner and other seafood victuals to be enjoyed on Young's spacious back patio with dozens of picnic tables or in the voluminous dining hall on the second floor. The whole operation sits on a wharf where lobster boats offload their catches throughout the day. You may witness firsthand the busy life

Young's does a brisk business shipping fresh seafood of all types overnight anywhere in the country. Check out their website to see the amazing variety of things they offer.

Top left: Young's cavernous building, as seen from the rear.

Above left: A couple of whimsical chairs out front.

Center: Capt. Seaweed.

Top right: The Bucket List for 2.

Above right: Rows of holding tanks for live lobsters.

of lobster wholesaling while taking in gorgeous views of Belfast Bay, the town of Belfast across the way, and in the distance, the grandeur of Penobscot Bay.

Young's menu is heavy on boiled lobster dinners of varying types, most served with butter, chips, and corn on the cob. Lobster stew and clam chowder are made fresh daily in the adjacent kitchen. Steamed clams, mussels, and shrimp are popular alternatives, as are several types of grilled fish fillets. There are no deep fryers at Young's.

The Young family has been running the lobster pound and restaurant since the 1930s, and they built the wharf in 1959. It's a great, busy, bustling place to learn more about the lobster trade and to have a wonderful lobster dinner at the same time.

2 Fairview St., East Belfast, 207-338-1160
youngslobsters.com

PIER FRENCH FRIES

An Old Orchard Beach classic

Old Orchard Beach has been a summertime playground for as long as anyone can remember. A carnival atmosphere presides over the downtown area, with lots of games arcades, amusement park rides, grab 'n' go eateries, and a large pier filled with shops, restaurants, bars, and more.

It's from this pier that Pier French Fries takes its name, since its original home was on the pier starting in 1932. Selling homemade fries made from hand-cut local spuds, Pier French Fries enjoyed a charmed life until 1969, when virtually the entire pier burned down. It was rebuilt, Pier Fries rose from the ashes, and lived a second life on the pier until the blizzard of 1978 destroyed the pier once again. Pier's third life found it in the market square located at the foot of the pier until 2002, when it moved across the street to its current location.

The eatery is a simple walk-up operation on a busy stretch of sidewalk, with a couple of service windows with blue-shirted staff ready to take your order. The menu is quite simple, though it's been tweaked a bit in recent years. At the core are the fries, which come in cup, pint, and box sizes, each larger than the other by a magnitude of two. When you place your order, it's filled almost immediately and handed to you right after you pay. This is street food in its most elemental, and Pier French Fries has become synonymous with summer in Old Orchard Beach.

Owners Tiffany and Allan Boutte preside over the stand, along with their son, Thomas. The potatoes come from New England and Canadian Maritime sources, and they reside in dozens of bags on pallets in the stand's back room. Each spud is carefully washed and peeled and then popped into an ancient, hand-operated cutter

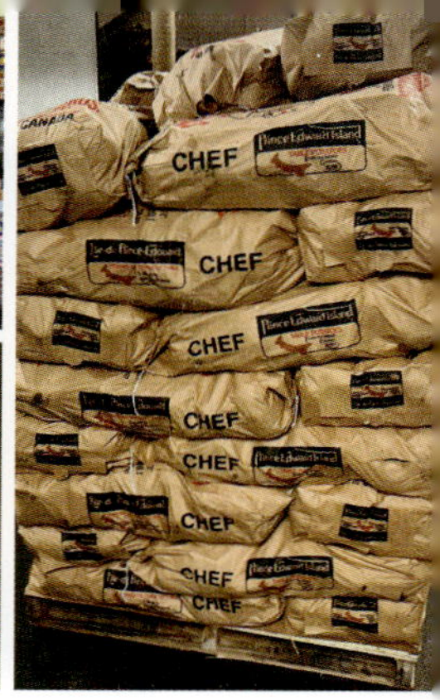

Left: A pint of fresh-cooked fries.

Left center: Baskets of fries ready to go.

Right center top: The busy order windows at Pier French Fries.

Right center above: Poutine.

Right: A fresh shipment of spuds in from Prince Edward Island.

that produces thousands of perfect crinkle-cut fries every day. Once cut, the uncooked fries are then placed in fryer baskets, which hang suspended next to the half-dozen fry-o-lators next to the order window. The whole operation is a marvel of efficiency.

Other menu offerings include steamed hot dogs, fried dough, and thick, gooey poutine, a popular French-Canadian dish consisting of french fries and chewy cheese curds bathed in rich, dark beef gravy. As to condiments for your cup or box of fries, there's the standard ketchup as well as, for many, the de rigueur dash of vinegar with a healthy sprinkling of salt. Let summer begin!

12 Old Orchard St., Old Orchard Beach, 207-934-2328
pierfrenchfries.com

The Bouttes purchased the adjacent Bill's Pizza stand in 2021. They're sticking with the original recipes and ingredients that have made this pizza spot, founded in 1949, another Orchard Beach institution.

ELSMERE BBQ AND WOOD GRILL

The pride and joy of South Portland

Back in 2013, when there was little in the way of barbecue in Maine, Elsmere BBQ and Wood Grill opened its doors in a former South Portland auto repair shop. This authentic barbecue joint is the brainchild of chefs and co-owners Adam Powers and Jeremy Rush, friends who have brought lots of love and barbecue knowledge to this thriving town.

Powers and Rush each developed a passion for barbecue before they met. Adam spent part of his youth in Southeast Asia, where he was fascinated by all of the types of casual, tasty street foods he encountered. He considers barbecue to be America's most unique form of street food, and he has been both a student and teacher of barbecuing for over 20 years. At one point, he created his own custom barbecue cooker out of a discarded 1950s metal refrigerator.

Jeremy, a Maine native, was exposed to barbecue on annual family visits to Kansas, one of the sacred grounds of American barbecue. His father pulled out the family smoker for special occasions, especially family gatherings. Jeremy's love and passion for barbecue have been with him ever since.

Elsmere is located in South Portland's Meeting House Hill neighborhood in what once was Ray's Auto Radiator shop. The original neon sign from the shop is illuminated behind the bar, a sight to behold. Also on display just inside the entryway is the wood grill with several stools overlooking the exposed part of the kitchen.

Elsmere prides itself in cooking and smoking with well-cured firewood, which is stored in an enclosed back garage. There are no natural gas starters or enhancers—just good, old-fashioned

Left: Smoked, grilled chicken wings.

Top center: The original auto repair shop sign graces the back of the bar.

Above center: A typical BBQ combo plate.

Top right: South Portland's pride and joy.

Above right: Counter seating by the wood grill.

woodsmoke flavor. Meats are smoked in a huge A. N. Bewley wood smoker from Texas, and all chicken and sausage grilling is done on an authentic Argentine wood grill.

Bell and Evans chicken is used for the wing and thigh dishes, smoked first and then finished on the grill. The smoker can hold several 30-pound pork butts and briskets, along with numerous slabs of St. Louis-style ribs, guaranteeing plenty of smoked meats.

Plates of barbecue come with a choice of sides such as collard greens, baked beans, coleslaw, cornbread, and mac and cheese, all homemade. And there are several types of salads and sandwiches for those who wish to go lighter.

Dine outdoors in season, if you wish, on the lovely patio and take in the street action of up-and-coming South Portland.

448 Cottage Rd., South Portland, 207-619-1948
elsmerebbq.com

There's another Elsmere location in the Deering Center neighborhood across the Fore River in neighboring Portland.

FURBISH BREW HOUSE & EATS

Great beer and pizza in a gorgeous mansion setting

There's been a culinary renaissance of sorts in the western mountain town of Rangeley over the past several years. One of the key drivers of that movement is Furbish Brew House & Eats, an eating and drinking establishment that has won near unanimous approval from townies and visitors drawn to the area's many year-round recreational activities.

Furbish is housed in an ornate mansion built in 1912 by local lumber and insurance magnate Harry Furbish, who oversaw construction of the original home and the formal gardens that were across the street. The house has been jacked up on a new foundation and is well elevated above street level, which allows for sweeping views of a lovely town park and Rangeley Lake.

For many years, the Furbish mansion served as an upscale bed and breakfast. Two couples, Ken and Amber Haley and Chip and Beth Smith, acquired the property and refurbished and retooled it to become the restaurant and microbrewery they envisioned.

Foremost in their plans, a wood-burning brick oven was installed in the kitchen, and cookers and fermenters were purchased to brew their own beers, ales, and stouts. They built a menu around these key elements, and they turned rooms on the first and second floors into dining areas and a barroom.

One of the most noticeable features of Furbish Brew House & Eats is its roomy, open-air brick patio out front with great views of the park and lake. It's a wonderful place to sit, relax, sip, and dine right in the center of town. Just inside the mansion's front door, a beautifully

Left: The grand entryway to Furbish Brew House & Eats.

Top center: The Furbish House Pizza.

Above center: Furbish's large outdoor patio.

Top right: Furbish's blueberry pilsner.

Above right: The wood-burning oven in the kitchen.

crafted wooden bar warmly greets all patrons. It's yet another great place to quaff some homemade brew and nibble on light eats and wood-fired pizza. Virtually all the dining areas upstairs and down have great views through large windows.

Pizza is what most folks go for, and with good reason. Furbish makes its own pizza dough and sauce fresh daily, and they use a custom mix of mozzarella and provolone cheeses on most of their pies. The Boston BBQ pork butt pizza is an eye-opener, with its blueberry-flavored barbecue sauce, and the Furbish House Pizza features a ricotta cheese base festooned with garlic, tomatoes, spinach, pine nuts, and a drizzle of balsamic glaze.

Come for Furbish's pizza and home-brewed beer. Linger for the view.

2541 Main St., Rangeley, 207-864-5847

The beers at Furbish are primarily of the fruity variety, with such offerings as blackberry blonde, strawberry oak wheat, chocolate stout, a blueberry pilsner, and the Furbish IPA, which is infused with a hint of grapefruit.

BOOTHBAY LOBSTER WHARF

A working lobster wharf with good views and great food

Located on the eastern shore of Boothbay Harbor, this venerable lobster wharf and pound has been doubling as a restaurant for some 20 years. Sitting on sturdy posts driven deep into the harbor floor, Boothbay Lobster Wharf is a great place to enjoy seafood with a great view of lobster boats coming and going as well as an excellent view of leisure craft and the quaint town of Boothbay Harbor across the way.

Some of the best lobster shacks are outgrowths of lobster piers and pounds, where fishermen offload their catches, and the dock owners bring the red guys to market. Such is the case with this place, which has seen a few different owners in the past two decades. Tom and Susan Philbrick are the current owners, having bought the wharf in 2016. They've maintained the wharf's brightly painted dock and tables, while lobster boats still pay daily visits to offload catches and pick up bait.

Step onto the pier, and you're greeted with steaming lobster pots and aquamarine tanks containing live lobsters of all sizes. You may pick your own or specify a weight and choose between hard shell and soft shell, and then seek out a picnic table on the expansive deck. Deep fried seafood and other goodies may be ordered at a separate window located in the wharf's small office building.

This is one of the best places to enjoy lobsters in Midcoast Maine, as the deck is open-air and offers a great place to dine al fresco. It hovers quite high above the waterline, though the prevailing tides lift boats closer to dock level a couple of times a day. You may witness the

Left: Lots of choices for lobster and more.

Top center: Boothbay Lobster Wharf's sturdy deck over the harbor waters.

Above center: Boothbay Lobster Wharf's famed lobster roll, with a side of lobster chowder.

Right: A crate of live lobsters, freshly arrived at the pound.

deck hands hoisting crates of freshly caught lobsters onto the dock using winches any time during the day.

Other menu highlights besides whole lobster and lobster dinners include the meaty lobster roll, mixed with generous amounts of mayo and served on a split-top bun with a plastic fork for the overflow. The deep fryers churn out crispy, golden pints and dinners of clams, clam strips, haddock, shrimp, and chicken fingers.

Should the weather turn nasty, there's a nifty, two-story enclosed dining area on the dock that sports a full bar and is the spot for live music on many summer nights. Lobster and other shellfish may also be packed up and taken live from the market for cooking at home.

97 Atlantic Ave., Boothbay Harbor, 207-633-4900
boothbaylobsterwharf.com

ABEL'S LOBSTER

One of the fine, old dining spots on Mount Desert Island

Somes Sound on Mount Desert Island is one of the prettiest, most serene bodies of water in Maine. It juts northward several miles from the Atlantic Ocean like a fjord into the island's interior. Those in the know who wish to take in the beauty of this splendid site while enjoying fine food and drink make their way to Abel's Lobster, a longtime favorite restaurant of well-heeled locals and numerous discriminating seasonal visitors.

Abel's is somewhat hidden behind a boatyard (also named Abel's) on the northeastern shore of the sound. A large sign on Route 3 indicates where to turn in, and then there are a few hairpin twists and turns heading down toward the water before the restaurant reveals itself.

The first thing you may notice is the stone, timber, and shingle chalet overlooking an outdoor cooking shed, picnic tables, fire rings, and pine trees, all with views of the water and the yachts docked next to the boatyard. It's an idyllic setting made even more appealing with the occasional appearances of bald eagles and other birds soaring overhead.

Abel's has been a lobster restaurant since the late 1930s, and for many years it was owned by two succeeding generations of the Stanley family. In June 2020, Mandy Fountaine, owner of nearby Bar Harbor Catering Company, bought Abel's and brought on seasoned New England chef Matt Leddy to help refine and establish a new menu from the kitchen. The dining areas have been refurbished, along with the menu, giving the old pound a refreshing new look and feel.

Patrons may dine indoors or out. The chalet features a lovely, pine-paneled dining room with large picture windows overlooking

Left: The indoor dining area.

Top center: Abel's chalet-like main building.

Above center: Abel's cozy barroom.

Top right: Scenic outdoor seating by Somes Sound.

Above right: A sack of lobsters going into the outdoor cooker.

the sound. There's also a cozy bar area with several stools for drinking or dining just inside the front door. The picnic tables outside are scattered over the evergreen-shaded grounds and offer perhaps the best water views.

The outdoor cooking shed is where lobsters are kept in cold-water tanks, and then cooked in pots filled with seawater over a wood-stoked fire. Oysters on the half shell, steamers, and a nice bibb salad are great starters. Fried clams and fish & chips are also available as entrees, and the meaty lobster roll is served on a brioche bun.

Lunch and dinner are both served at this seasonal beauty on the splendid shores of Somes Sound.

13 Abels Lane, Mount Desert, 207-276-8221
abelslobstermdi.com

MAINE LOBSTER FESTIVAL

Five days of complete lobster immersion

Having just celebrated its 75th anniversary in 2022, the Maine Lobster Festival lives on in the hearts and minds (and appetites) of Mainers and folks "from away." It also continues to serve as a focal point for the most prominent industry in Midcoast Maine: lobstering.

Staged in Rockland's Harbor Park on the town's waterfront, the festival is five days of fun that features live music, arts and crafts, parades, beauty contest coronations, events for kids, and most important, lobster served in every form imaginable.

In 1947, not long after the end of World War II, town leaders in Camden, Rockport, and Rockland got together and started planning ways to celebrate the maritime culture of the region, both to lift local spirits and to attract tourists to the region. The concept rapidly turned into the Maine Lobster Festival, paying homage to the large, local lobster-fishing community and serving up fresh-caught Maine lobster, the pride and joy of the Midcoast region. The festival has grown steadily over the years, attracting visitors from all over the country, from Canada, and even from overseas.

So, what's to eat at this five-day extravaganza? The most popular item is, of course, the lobster dinner, which features your choice of one, two, or (gasp) three 1 ¼-pound cooked lobsters,

Be sure to check out the World's Largest Lobster Cooker, a gargantuan setup of half a dozen large boilers into which hundreds of lobsters at a time are immersed and cooked to perfection.

Left: The Lobster Café, for lobster roll fans.
Left center: The lobster dinner with a side of seafood chowder.
Right center top: The main float in the Lobster Festival parade.
Right center above: Fried dough is one of many food trailers at the festival.
Right: A crate of freshly cooked lobsters emerging from the cooker.

accompanied by an ear of fresh corn on the cob and a cup of melted butter. The basic dinner may be upgraded to a Maine Shore Dinner, which is a lobster dinner augmented with steamed clams, a cup of clam chowder, and coleslaw. Line up in front of the main food tent to place your order, get and pay for your victuals, and then grab a seat in the communal dining area under the tent, where there's live music.

Other dishes available in the main food tent include lobster mac and cheese, lobster bisque, steamed mussels, and four different types of chowder. An adjacent Lobster Café serves up meaty lobster rolls, lobster Caesar wraps, and a healthy lobster Caesar salad. For those shunning seafood altogether, check out the many food trucks parked throughout the fairgrounds, where such treats as fried chicken, Italian sub sandwiches, fried dough, and ice cream may be procured.

Midcoast Maine takes pride in its lobster heritage, and the Maine Lobster Festival is a great way to celebrate all things lobster in early August every year.

1 Pleasant St., Rockland, 800-576-7512
mainelobsterfestival.com

THE COFFEE POT SANDWICH

A legendary sandwich lives on in the Queen City of the East

In the early morning of December 31, 2009, a line began to form in front of the Coffee Pot restaurant on State Street in downtown Bangor. By mid-morning, the line numbered several hundred people and stretched down State Street, farther continuing onto nearby Boyd Street. Why? Coffee Pot owner Skip Rist was shuttering the restaurant after that day in order to retire, and diehard fans of the Coffee Pot's signature sandwich were desperate for one last bite.

The Coffee Pot sandwich had been legendary in Bangor ever since the restaurant started selling them in 1930. Generations grew up on Coffee Pot grub, and clearly the restaurant was going to be missed. An atmosphere of nostalgia, sadness, and even desperation settled in over those waiting in line. Sandwiches were selling for as much as 10 times the retail price between scalpers and wannabe customers. Requests came in from around the country to try and score one last Coffee Pot sandwich.

The story doesn't end there. Shortly after the Coffee Pot was shuttered, several enterprising restaurateurs stepped into the breach and began selling their own Coffee Pot sandwiches. Two of those restaurants: the newly opened "Coffee Pot" restaurant on Broadway just off I-95, and the Legacy sandwich shop, located next door to the spot of the original Coffee Pot on State Street.

What makes the Coffee Pot sandwich so special? For starters, it's served on a short, soft Italian roll split down the top with a bread knife. The interior is packed with chopped raw onion, green pepper, tomato slices, salt, salad oil dressing, and a dash of red pepper flakes. Layered on top of the basic sandwich are slices of salami, American cheese, and half a dozen pickle slices. The whole

Top left: Coffee Pot sandwiches ready for sale.
Above left: A Legacy Coffee Pot sandwich under construction.
Top center: The menu at the Coffee Pot on Broadway.
Above center: The Legacy Sandwich Shop on State Street.
Right: The Legacy's Coffee Pot sandwich.

thing is tightly wrapped in waxed paper for easy transport and to serve as a resting place between bites.

Each of the restaurants have numerous variations and add-ons to the basic Coffee Pot sandwich, such as different types of cheeses and salami, ham, tuna, roast beef, turkey, banana peppers, capicola, chicken salad, and straight-up veg. You may dine in or carry out; both options are equally popular.

Bangor is lucky and smart to keep this culinary tradition alive. Get yourself a Coffee Pot sandwich and see what Bangor has been enjoying for nearly 100 years.

Coffee Pot Sandwich Shop
652 Broadway, Bangor,
207-990-2633
thecoffeepotbangor.com

Legacy Sandwich Shop
163 State St., Bangor,
207-974-3085

ALLAGASH BREWING

Wheat beer and lobster rolls—a winning combination

There are hundreds of microbreweries in Maine, and one of the best known and most successful is Portland's Allagash Brewing Company. From modest beginnings as a one-person operation in 1995, Allagash has grown exponentially into an award-winning beermaker of national, even international, renown. And you may visit their brewery on the western fringes of Portland to enjoy some of their beers and to feast on some great food to boot.

The Allagash story began when incipient brewer Rob Tod struck out on his own in 1995, opening a small brewing operation inside a Portland warehouse. He came up with the name "Allagash" for his brewery, and he started with a Belgian-style wheat beer that he named Allagash White. It was quite different from what Portlanders were used to quaffing, but after a while the brew, spiced with coriander and orange peel, garnered a loyal following. Vermont brewer Jason Perkins joined Allagash in 1999, and the brewery has been on a roll ever since.

The look and feel of today's brewery grounds are that of a beer garden, with numerous tables, chairs, umbrellas, and sheltered areas scattered around the grounds of Allagash's expansive facilities. Fermentation tanks form the backdrop for the outdoor scene, towering 30 feet or more above the beer garden below. The grounds are also graced with several colorful murals and posters heralding the brewing and drinking of fine beers and the glories of living in Maine.

Upon entering the grounds, most visitors make a beeline to the numerous taps displayed behind the front-and-center, stand-up bar to select one of the many brews. In addition to Allagash White and the Belgian pale ale, there are several rotating brews on draught, such as sour ales, IPAs, dark lagers, and fruit-enhanced libations. The knowledgeable barkeeps can explain what's available.

Top left: Bite Into Maine's food trailer is a permanent fixture.

Above left: A couple of glasses of famed Allagash White.

Top center: Founder Rob Tod. Courtesy Allagash Brewing Company

Above center: One of many murals in Allagash's beer garden.

Right: A warm greeting from Allagash Brewing.

Step inside the store next to the tap stand, where several coolers beckon with six- and 12-packs of various Allagash brews available for purchase to take home. Bottle and can pours featuring some of the brewery's best limited-edition beers are also available from the store's coolers.

Hungry? Lucky for you because Bite Into Maine, the famed lobster roll purveyor, has an Airstream trailer permanently parked in the beer garden.

This is a great place to spend an afternoon or early evening during the warm, sunny summer months, enjoying fine beers, great seafood, and a wonderful atmosphere of camaraderie in a European-style beer garden setting.

50 Industrial Way, Portland, 207-330-5385
allagash.com

Allagash Brewing Company has won seven gold medals in national and international competitions in the past 25 years as well as several silver and bronze winners.

PEMAQUID SEAFOOD

Great lobster, even better views

What was once known as the Pemaquid Lobster Cooperative is now the independently owned Pemaquid Seafood Restaurant. The differences between the two are subtle, but the lobster's still great, and the views of the Pemaquid River and the harbor beyond are still fantastic.

Finding Pemaquid Seafood calls for driving down narrow roads through nicely landscaped residential areas until you get close, and then a long driveway to the eatery turns to dirt. Follow it down to a parking lot and a modest shack perched on a hilltop overlooking the river. The magnificence of the view doesn't reveal itself until you walk around the shack and step onto the recently constructed deck covered with picnic tables and umbrellas. It's a great place to enjoy some lobster in an amazing setting.

The Pemaquid Lobster Cooperative was formed in 1947 by local fishermen in Bristol, Maine. They pooled their resources, shipped out daily from the same dock, and returned with their catch, which was pooled together as a co-op and then sold inland to wholesalers and retailers such as restaurants and seafood markets. A somewhat primitive, cinder-block eatery was constructed next to the co-op in 1987. Curious locals and adventurous tourists started showing up to enjoy freshly boiled lobster at picnic tables scattered around the grounds.

Step inside today's screened shack, where you may place your order or grab a table if the weather isn't behaving. (Dining on

The lobster co-op still exists and may be visited at the bottom of the hill. Both are owned by the Simmons family.

Top left: Pemaquid's food shack.

Above left: Digging in.

Center: The Harbor Platter.

Top right: The amazing view from Pemaquid's deck.

Above right: This sign lets you know you've found the place.

the deck is by far the better way to go.) Pemaquid is a dine-in-the-rough operation, so you order your food through the interior window on the left and pick it up through the window on the right. Everything is listed on a large, colorful blackboard, and it's virtually all seafood, befitting of its rural maritime setting.

Whole lobster is served as single, twin, and triple lobster dinners, each accompanied by an ear of steamed corn still in its husk, coleslaw, a dinner roll, and the obligatory cup or two of melted butter. Or you may order the Harbor Platter, which consists of a 1 ¼-pound lobster, corn, slaw, butter, and a pound of steamer clams accompanied by broth. Cold lobster rolls are available in small and large sizes.

Unlike many other Midcoast lobster pounds, Pemaquid has deep fryers, serving up fried clams, strips, scallops, and shrimp. Each fried dinner includes fries, coleslaw, and a roll. There's something for everyone at this pretty little spot.

32 Co-Op Rd., Pemaquid, 207-667-2642
pemaquidseafood.com

SPRING CREEK BAR-B-Q

Real-deal smoked goods near the Appalachian Trail

Barbecue joints have been popping up all over Maine in the past several years, but few have the longevity or bona fide barbecue street cred of Spring Creek Bar-B-Q in the town of Monson. Founded in 2000 by Mike and Kim Witham, this unique, casual spot has won a big following among locals as well as that of hikers on the nearby Appalachian Trail.

In 1999, Mike and Kim, who met cooking on the local festivals circuit, purchased a modest house on Monson's Main Street and started converting it into what would be the only restaurant in Monson at that time. They began by cooking and serving barbecue from a stand in front of the building, garnering lots of attention.

They have since moved to larger quarters in another house up the street from their original location. Mike's two smokers sit proudly on the side porch, where he often sits in a chair and chats with customers as they come and go. Kim handles much of the kitchen work, assembling orders for customers, while Mike preps the meats with his special dry rubs in the kitchen and smokes them outside.

Enter Spring Creek through the front (actually side) door, and you'll encounter the order window. The menu appears on a series of small chalkboards spread around the window, so study these first before stepping up and ordering. Kim will most likely be the one taking your order. (This is a true mom-and-pop place.)

One of the most popular items is the BBQ pork sandwich, a hefty offering served on a bun or in a cup, if you wish to go without bread. It's garnished with raw onion and pickles and comes wrapped in tin foil. The smoked chicken salad sandwich is also

Top left: Spring Creek's nicely appointed dining room.

Above left: Slabs of ribs, fresh out of the smokers.

Top center: The order window with Kim Witham working away in the kitchen.

Above center: Spring Creek Bar-B-Q, as seen from the street.

Right: The pulled pork sandwich with homemade macaroni salad.

popular and comes on a roll or in a cup. Another longtime favorite of regulars is Mike and Kim's homemade sausage, assembled in the kitchen and thrown on the smoker until juicy and fragrant.

Though much of Spring Creek's business is takeout, there's a lovely, wood-paneled dining room with varnished tables made of rough-hewn wood. The small bar, manned by Mike, is similarly constructed and a nice place to grab a draft or other libation. Several tables sit just outside the porch for fair-weather dining. All in all, it's a great way to start (or finish) a visit to the Moosehead Lake region to the north.

26 Greenville Rd., Monson, 207-997-7025

Spring Creek keeps unpredictable days and hours of operation, one of their hallmarks. As owner Mike Witham likes to say, "If you smell good things coming from our smokers, then you know we're open."

CLAWS

A lobster shack with a sense of humor

Rockland claims to be the lobster capital of the world, and it hosts the Maine Lobster Festival every August, a townwide event that draws tens of thousands of lobster lovers. So it's a bit surprising that for many years Rockland didn't really have a bona fide lobster shack. That was remedied when Claws opened its doors in 2014 and immediately became a magnet for seafood lovers from Rockland and beyond.

Claws is the brainchild of Steve and Luann Stinson, both of whom have roots in the Maine seafood industry. Steve's family owned a sardine cannery in Belfast for many years, and Luann's father fished for herring in the Gulf of Maine. The two decided to open a dine-in-the-rough seafood restaurant in an area that needed one, and they hit upon Rockland as their target.

Claws is as much a feast for the eyes as it is for the palate. Painted bright lobster-red and situated on busy Route 1 just north of downtown Rockland, this place is hard to miss and a shame to pass by without stopping. In addition to the reddish hue, there are old-fashioned wooden lobster traps on the roof, a bait barrel with fake fisherman's legs sticking up out of it, lots of buoys and ropes and lobster props strung out all over the property, and a large sign by the order window declaring "WELCOME TO ROCKLAND, MAINE, LOBSTER CAPITAL OF THE WORLD."

Although carryout is available, it's far better to dine on the premises, as there's a covered deck area and porch with great views of Rockland's working harbor and the famed Rockland Breakwater Lighthouse. You may watch commercial and pleasure craft come and go while you dine. There's also a rosy-red dining area with several tables next to busy Route 1.

Left: The airy deck overlooking the harbor.

Top center: A bit of whimsy by the order window.

Above center: This sign's message is clear.

Top right: A Claws's lobster roll, dusted with paprika.

Above right: Claws screams lobster.

The menu at Claws offers amazing variety for a lobster shack, though lobster in all of its variations forms the core of the menu. Their Hot and Crabby Artichoke Dip is a great starter. Also consider the Greek-inspired calamari, garnished with banana peppers, capers, kalamata olives, and feta cheese.

The lobster rolls come in quarter-pound, half-pound, and full-pound sizes, each one in appropriate-sized buns. The whole-lobster dinners come in various configurations with sides such as corn, steamers, coleslaw, blueberry biscuits, and of course, warm drawn butter.

Deep-fried seafood and a variety of seafood-stuffed tacos round out the amazing offerings at this welcome addition to the Rockland dining scene. Check it out.

743 Main St., Rockland, 207-596-5600
clawsrocklandmaine.com

TRENTON BRIDGE LOBSTER POUND

Roadside cookers pull in the hungry and the curious

As you approach the Route 3 bridge that leads from Ellsworth to Mount Desert Island and Acadia National Park, you come across an otherworldly sight: half a dozen tin chimneys spewing woodsmoke skyward from roadside cookers in front of a small, whitewashed seafood stand. If you feel even the slightest bit peckish, you should pull into the parking lot and order up some lobster at Trenton Bridge Lobster Pound, one of the premier lobster eateries in Maine's Acadia region.

Trenton Bridge Lobster got its start in 1956 when George and Gertrude Gascon bought Ogden Lobster Pound, which sat next to the bridge leading to Thompson and Mount Desert Islands. The Gascons poured their love and a significant amount of their savings into the pound, keeping the focus of the place on selling and cooking live, locally caught lobsters. Over the next 40 years, a succession of owners, all of whom descended from the maternal side of the Gascon family, kept the place going. As traffic to Mount Desert Island and the park grew, so did the business for the pound. Current owners, Anthony and Josette Pettegrow, and their son, Warren, are third- and fourth-generation family members currently in charge of the restaurant.

Things at the pound have remained simple over the decades of operation. Fresh-caught lobsters are boiled in sea water heated by wood-fired outdoor cookers lined up between the shack and the parking lot. Trenton Bridge claims this is the best way to prepare lobsters.

Top left: The Trenton Bridge team, ready to take your order.

Above left: Perfectly cooked lobsters fresh from the pot.

Top right: The famed, wood-burning outdoor cookers.

Above right: Trenton Bridge's inviting façade.

Dining at Trenton Bridge is a feast for the senses. First, there are the outdoor cookers on display as you stroll from the parking lot to the brightly painted shack. Once inside, you're invited to pick your own lobster from one of the holding tanks and select any other items you may wish to have from Trenton Bridge's menu. Your lobster is put into a netted sack and taken to the cookers outside while you find a place to sit at one of the many picnic tables around the side and back of the building. Then there's the unforgettable aroma of fresh-cooked lobster when your order is ready.

In addition to whole lobster, Trenton Bridge offers hot (buttered) and cold lobster rolls, a lobster salad sandwich, lobster stew, and a dinner salad covered with lobster meat. Corn on the cob and potato salad are popular sides, and the home-baked blueberry pie is not to be missed.

1237 Bar Harbor Rd., Trenton, 207-667-2977
trentonbridgelobster.com

ROCK'S FAMILY DINER

The place that whoopie pies made famous

This modest eatery is famous for two things: its location at the beginning of US Route 1 (which winds its way south all the way to Key West, Florida) and for its nationally famous whoopie pies.

The story began in 1945 when high schooler Rock Oullette opened a part-time hot dog stand, and then pretty quickly converted it into a full-time restaurant after the end of World War II. Its location across the street from the US International Port of Entry bridge spanning the St. John River between the United States and Canada guaranteed a steady stream of traffic going both ways for many years.

The one-story, red-colored building radiates a warmth inside, with pine-paneled walls, a counter with stools, and a couple of spacious dining rooms that can accommodate nearly a hundred people. There's always lots of friendly banter between locals and patrons from away, as folks exchange tales from the road and the latest town news.

Current owners, Peter and Sandra Pinette, have been at the helm since 2001. They pride themselves in feeding the local community as well as weary travelers, and in providing a place where friends and family can gather, share a meal or a cup of coffee, and swap stories.

The menu is pretty straightforward, with hot dogs still selling strong after all these years, followed closely by burgers in various styles. There's an abbreviated breakfast menu for early risers as well as such Franco-American favorites like the Lumberjack Poutine, a healthy serving of french fries bathed in rich gravy and topped with cheese curds.

Left: Rock's Diner, with a couple of rocks in the front yard.
Center: There's always fresh-baked whoopie pies ready for sale on Rock's counter.
Right: Rock's famous pumpkin whoopie pie.

Homemade whoopie pies have always been a specialty here, dating back more than 40 years and baked up fresh daily in the diner's large kitchen. In addition to the traditional chocolate whoopie pies with cream filling, there are pumpkin and chocolate chip varieties and a chocolate version with peanut butter filling.

During the pandemic, fans of Rock's whoopie pies had them delivered by the dozen, a welcome form of comfort food during trying times. One customer in New York ordered 12 dozen to hand out to stressed-out New York City health care workers, an act of kindness that went viral on the internet. Thousands of orders followed, and in no time requests for the tasty treats had come from all 50 states.

Rock's is a classic example of a simple eatery that its community has come to rely on for good food, great company, and a port in the storm during difficult times.

378 West Main St., Fort Kent, 207-834-2888
rocksfamilydiner.com

THE LOST KITCHEN

Maine's mystical, mythical holy grail of eateries

The Lost Kitchen should win the award for most unique eatery in Maine. It's also the most difficult place (perhaps in the entire country) to get a reservation. The story of this amazing restaurant is inextricably tied to its creator, owner, and cook, Erin French. Rising from the ashes of a life that she thought she could no longer bear, this resilient, determined, thoughtful, loving, and driven woman almost single-handedly took lemons and turned them into champagne.

French was born and raised in the tiny town of Freedom, Maine, population 700, located some 20 miles west of Belfast. She had some early experience cooking at her father's diner before leaving for college in Boston and a planned medical career. An accidental pregnancy derailed those plans, followed by a failed restaurant and marriage in Belfast, in turn followed by addiction and recovery.

Back in her hometown and living with her parents, French, a self-taught cook, continued to hone her skills, focusing on simple dishes using fresh local ingredients. She started a pop-up dinner business out of a converted Airstream trailer, and then had an epiphany when she visited Freedom's old, crumbling grist mill. She envisioned the beautiful, timber-frame, high-ceilinged dining room with open kitchen that constitute the Lost Kitchen today. It's a place where Erin can ply her skills, assisted by her mother and her crew of local women, some of whom are farmers who also supply the eatery with fresh meat, produce, and dairy.

The wood-hewn tables and chairs have been crafted from local reclaimed lumber and perfectly match the ambience of the mill setting. A nicely curated gift shop, featuring home goods, fine wines, and copies of Erin's cookbook and memoir, is open on a limited basis but well worth the visit, should you wish to stroll the grounds, see the mill building, and check out the Airstream trailer, which sits astride a patio area.

Left: There's a small patio area next to the pretty mill pond.

Center: The Lost Kitchen recently opened a gift shop featuring fine home goods.

Top right: The Airstream trailer that Erin French transformed into a rolling kitchen.

Above right: The Lost Kitchen, housed in a rehabbed mill in Freedom, Maine.

The season is short, from May to October, and dinner is served four nights per week to some 48 lucky guests. The menu changes each day, depending on what Erin and her staff harvest from local fields and the nearby fisheries of Midcoast Maine. The results are said to be consistently amazing.

How to get a reservation? You send in a postcard with your contact information, and starting in April each year, the staff randomly pulls cards out of a pile to determine who will receive invites. There are currently more than 50,000 postcards in the pile, with more coming every day. So, the chances may be slim, but hope springs eternal in Freedom, Maine!

22 Mill St., Freedom
findthelostkitchen.com

Want to submit a reservation postcard? Instructions for how and when to submit and what information to provide on the card may be found on the "Reservations" link located on the Lost Kitchen's website.

Moody's Diner

RESTAURANTS A-Z

Five Islands Lobster Company

CO.

Susan's Fish & Chips

APPENDIX

SOUTHERN COAST

GREATER PORTLAND

MIDCOAST

PENOBSCOT BAY

ACADIA

DOWNEAST

CENTRAL AND WESTERN MAINE

NORTHERN MAINE